TRUMP
The Ultimate Contrarian

Richard Alston

DONALD TRUMP

The Ultimate Contrarian

Richard Alston

Connor Court Publishing Pty Ltd

Connor Court Publishing Pty Ltd.

PO Box 7257

Redland Bay QLD 4165

sales@connorcourt.com

www.connorcourt.com

ISBN: 9781922449832

Cover Design by Maria Giordano

Printed in Australia.

Front Cover Photo: Donald Trump speaking at the 2018 Conservative Political Action Conference (CPAC) in National Harbor, Maryland, by Gage Skidmore, (Commons Wikimedia)

Contents

Introduction

As Joe Biden approaches the end of his first year in the White House his prospects at the 2022 midterms are not looking good and his chances of re-election in 2024 are increasingly remote.

By then he will be well into his 80s, his cognitive capability is most unlikely to have improved and there will be no sympathy vote.

It will be very surprising if he does run again – he might not even get the nomination. This will not stop him from keeping his options open, so as not to be prematurely seen as a lame duck.

In the wake of the Kabul exit fiasco, and his determination to drown the American economy and taxpayers in debt, he is increasingly being seen as not just weak and befuddled, but on the wrong track.

The heir apparent, Kamala Harris, is doing little better and is unlikely to prove a winner if Biden chooses not to run. She lacks both experience and gravitas and has little connection with middle America.

But the fact that Trump is currently well ahead in the polls does not mean that he will necessarily be the candidate next time or even that he should be.

It may also be a somewhat different Donald Trump next time. His fundamental values and policy instincts are well known so he will only need to campaign on his brand, without the hyper aggression and needless offensiveness which clearly alienated some erstwhile supporters in 2020.

His successor has, not surprisingly, proved to be his polar opposite – but not necessarily for the better.

Most Americans who voted for Joe Biden thought that they were getting a moderate, in keeping with his lifelong political track record, but, instead, what they have ended up with is a slightly less strident version of Bernie Sanders' socialist dream, which most Americans don't want. Biden is now seen as a prisoner of the left, even though he has never belonged there.

While there are no obvious viable Democrat successors, there are a number of impressive candidates on the Republican side, waiting in the wings.

These include Nikki Haley, Mike Pompeo, Marco Rubio, Ron DeSantis, Tom Cotton and Mike Pence.

If they can craft a Trump-light series of policies on families and jobs, together with tough border and immigration, they might have a show.

Each of them is smart enough to realise that the Donald's trump card was catering for the needs and aspirations of ordinary working class Americans, who had been neglected too much for too long.

But they will need to play their cards shrewdly – any sign of overt disloyalty to the front runner will result in them being instantly anathematised.

This essay is therefore devoted to identifying those concrete achievements and policy initiatives of Donald Trump, which could be seen to be the key to not only electoral success but getting America back on track.

If the next president is willing and able to adopt Trump's winning formula and re-set America on its winning ways, then Donald Trump will have earned his place in history.

The ultimate test of Trump's legacy will be whether his achievements prove to be transitory or permanent, à la Margaret Thatcher. But either way it would be very shortsighted to ignore the merits of many of his policy prescriptions.

1

Threading the Eye of the Needle

History teaches us that flawed individuals and policy processes sometimes produce successful results

– Robert D. Blackwill,
Henry A. Kissinger senior fellow for US foreign policy

History will rightly judge that Donald Trump's term as President of the United States ended in disgrace. His outrageous post-election behaviour, his refusal to admit defeat, and his pretence that somehow the electoral process had been rigged, incited a mob invasion of the Capitol building, the political holy of holies in Washington, DC.

Even his most rational supporters would be hard-pressed to deny that, although he was an eccentric high achiever who still had a magnetic attraction to a huge number of people, his actions in ensuring that the Republican Party lost both Georgia seats in the Senate in the run-off rightly earn him political vilification, not only from his own side but from the American people, whose earlier voting patterns had strongly indicated that they did not want to see Joe Biden given a blank cheque, as has now effectively happened.

If Trump were to be judged solely on character there is little doubt that he would be at the bottom of the class. But, if the criterion is performance in office, he may get a much higher score. It has been a long-standing sport amongst historians and political scientists to rank presidents, but always on the basis of what they achieved in office, not what character deficiencies they displayed.

JFK still has a large fan club, despite his flagrant moral laxity. His successor was even worse. Lyndon Johnson was, from most reports, an odious character in personal terms, yet he is still widely celebrated for his historic achievements in putting in place the *Civil Rights Act*, and, to a lesser extent, for his attempt to deliver The Great Society.

In the current political climate, it is almost impossible to find anyone to say a good word about Donald Trump. This is perfectly understandable, as he is a very unattractive human being. In addition, his manner of communicating and his methods of decision-making were often bizarre in the extreme, providing many millions with sufficient evidence to dismiss not just the man, but his policy achievements.

There is little point in attempting to retrieve the personal reputation of a deeply flawed human being. A much more productive responsibility would be to look closely at his achievements in office with a view to identifying and learning from those that were successful.

Chaos theory argues that, within the apparent randomness of complex systems, there can be coherent patterns, interconnectedness and constant feedback loops.

Loosely applied to Donald Trump, it suggests that, beneath the underlying structure of his disorganised speech, behaviour and apparently random thought processes, there was a set of lucid policy objectives which could be applied to fixing the economy and rebuilding the nation. Perhaps there was method in his madness!

While the devastating impact of the coronavirus will have a long-lasting impact on American society, and add further colour to the Trump era, the sober judgment of history may well be that Donald Trump's period as President of the United States was very consequential. In many ways, as geo-political expert Greg Sheridan has written, he redefined conservative politics throughout the Western world, in the face of ferocious opposition. Fortunately, like Reagan and Thatcher, he was never deterred.

Unfortunately and unnecessarily, he thrived on being nasty, vindictive, aggressive, offensive and tough as nails. Ultimately his demise was due to self-inflicted injuries, and lack of any sense of balance, but, by the time he left the stage, he had racked up more positive achievements than many of his predecessors.

History will probably decide that one term was enough – by then he had done his job. His pyrotechnics had inflamed too many and worn out some of even his most fervent erstwhile supporters. But to leave office having garnered more than 74 million votes is a breathtaking achievement in the face of overwhelming and unrelenting antipathy from the media, the elites, academics, the business community and millions of educated city dwellers, and one that will ensure an everlasting larger-than-life imprint on American politics.

The ferocity of Trump's attacks on his opponents, even early in his term of office, provoked vitriolic counter-attacks from a legion of members of a rapidly formed "resistance", as well as self-proclaimed Never Trumpers in the Republican ranks. As a result, politics in America rapidly degenerated into a brutal and, at times, hysterical, blood feud.

Whether he has made America great again is too early to judge, but there is no doubt he has changed the fabric of American society, showing how to revive the national economy, reanimating the entrepreneurial spirit, and giving the masses the confidence to believe in themselves once again.

His electoral loss can be largely attributed to coarse and often outrageous personal behaviour, which ultimately offended too many. And by allowing his personality, not his achievements, to become the issue, he handed Joe Biden a winning hand. The election became a character preference instead of a choice between competing policy offerings.

In my view the single biggest reason for his ultimate electoral failure was his inability to change gears from opposition, where much more is tolerated, to government where much more is expected – like a punch drunk boxer he just kept throwing punches wildly, indiscriminately and eventually counter-productively.

But despite his ultimately fatal divisive governance and gross personal shortcomings, his infectious enthusiasm for life and his determination to disrupt the existing order were like a breath of fresh air to millions. His rallies attracted a rock star following of enthusiastic converts, exhilarated by his political bravery. His accomplishments therefore bear close examination.

When he came to office, after eight slow growth Obama-led years, the combined state and federal taxation rate on corporate profits was nearly 40%, the highest in the industrialised world, with a corresponding dampening effect on competition and employment, causing many large corporations to flee offshore to lower tax environments.

His *Tax Cuts and Jobs Act* reduced the top federal corporate tax rate from 35% to 21% and, together with his stroke of genius in enticing the repatriation of literally trillions of dollars in capital, triggered a massive increase in domestic business investment and a commensurate expansion in job creation.

What is often forgotten is that his policies also helped minorities – prison reform, opportunity zones, support for alternatives to failing public schools.

His delivered on his promise to "drain the swamp" by cutting through acres of bureaucratic red tape. This proved particularly valuable in speeding up major infrastructure projects in another area where his firsthand business experience proved invaluable.

Another of his most enduring legacies is likely to be his success in securing the appointment of more than 200 federal court judges, as well as three critically important lifetime appointments to the Supreme Court, in the face of often ferocious opposition.

The foreign policy arena was probably the last place anyone expected Trump to shine. He had no demonstrated aptitude, let alone experience, in a notoriously sensitive arena, where words are bullets and most tread very warily. He had spent a lifetime glued to home turf and had shown no interest in expanding his horizons. Yet he turned out to be a bold and revolutionary trailblazer, overturning many shibboleths and slaughtering many sacred cows along the way.

Particularly important were his breakthrough achievements in the Middle East, the graveyard of many presidential aspirations. By bringing together Israel and a number of its erstwhile enemies, particularly in the Gulf and Africa, to understand the practical trading and other benefits to be derived from burying long-standing enmities, he transformed, hopefully permanently, the Middle East equation, which had been quagmired for decades. His decision to move the US embassy to Jerusalem was an allied game-changer, leading to a major breakthrough in Arab-Israeli relations.

Standing up to the long-standing unwillingness of NATO countries to pull their weight in defence spending, by threatening to withdraw from the alliance, was a classic Trump play.

By ripping up Obama's soft and deeply flawed nuclear deal he put Iran on the backfoot and his punitive tariffs hit that country's economy hard, limiting its capacity for mischief-making in the region. The laser-like killing of one of its top military commanders was a chilling demonstration of the US's continuing military prowess, but, more importantly, its willingness to act decisively when a major opportunity presented itself.

Trump is a very unusual political animal – in personal terms he is a brutish vulgarian. Even admirers, like *The Australian*'s Chris Kenny, are quick to describe him as unorthodox, polarising and crass. But, as Kenny also points out, we knew all this four years ago. Boorish behaviour does not necessarily disqualify from being an effective president.

Many of his predecessors had personal shortcomings. Andrew Jackson, a war hero and founder of the Democratic Party, not only shot a man in cold blood in the course of one of his many duels, but, on his deathbed, said of two of his political opponents that his only regrets were that he did not "shoot Henry Clay or murder John Calhoun".

Jackson biographer, Robert V. Remini, said that he was "a terrible, vindictive enemy" to the Indians against whom he waged war, and that his treatment of his own slaves "can only be described as barbaric". He was nevertheless twice elected president and is now often rated among the top ten best presidents.

So, if Trump had managed to get away with his outsized and often outrageous persona four years ago and was headed for victory, what changed in 2020?

The short answer is that he overplayed his hand.

What the American middle class wanted, after being treated as "deplorables" for most of the previous decade, was someone who would take their concerns seriously – particularly about out of control illegal immigration, jobs-destroying trade, and a declining standard of living. They accepted that the media was untrustworthy, and had treated Trump disgracefully, and did not mind him giving them a big serve. But they did not particularly like the endless torrent of mostly unnecessary abuse of all and sundry that went with it.

I suspect that there were just enough who were grateful for his achievements but could not quite stomach the thought of four more years of confected mayhem, to have made the difference between winning and losing. In many ways, he had broken the dam wall and they would forever be grateful, but enough was enough.

His handling of the corona virus issue was far from exemplary. Like a number of others he did not take it seriously at the outset, believing it would soon blow over. At times his cavalier insouciance jarred with commentators, although I suspect that ordinary Americans knew that the greatest danger was a job-destroying locked-down economy. They saw him as someone trying to put a positive spin on things and not as someone unconcerned about their health.

Exit polls seem to indicate that Americans did not hold him responsible for his handling of the virus. Like many others elsewhere he was working in the dark on a unique challenge for which no one was politically prepared, and he probably performed better than a number of state governors.

More than 63 million people voted for Trump in 2016, including millions of women, many of whom may have held their noses while doing so, but preferred him to the do-nothing alternative.

In the lead-up to the 2016 election, Trump was universally regarded as a rank outsider with little hope of beating the formidable Clinton machine. Yet he triumphed against the odds. With more than 74 million votes in 2020 he nearly did it again.

Trump is *sui generis* – he thrived on turbulence, confrontation and, above all, disruption, as much a political strategy as an instinctive behavioural characteristic. There is no other politician remotely like him – disdainful of others, the polar opposite of the smooth and articulate whitebread candidate from central casting, nakedly political, demanding to be judged by his firm and decisive actions rather than his language and behavioural crudities.

For most politicians words can be dangerous weapons, normally aimed at a specific target. Trump preferred the opposite, happy to unleash a torrential spray, not really concerned with the accuracy of his statements.

Yet, in the midst of seeming chaos, with top-level staffers and advisers coming and going with extraordinary rapidity, he achieved a number of significant successes which have been of direct benefit to ordinary Americans. He also did his best to honour all his campaign promises, and largely succeeded.

Voters knew what you got with an unvarnished Trump – notoriously thin-skinned, yet adamantine in pursuit of his key objectives. They also identified with his positive, can-do approach.

More fundamentally, Trump showed that focusing on the economic well-being of the majority can be a winning strategy. For those who pine for a softer, gentler program, they should reflect on whether it should be at the expense of an effective economic and financial agenda.

One of the most extraordinary outcomes of the 2020 election was the switch in voting behaviour of many blacks and Latinos. Viewed purely from a race perspective, Trump did not do much to endear himself to non-white voters. Yet many of these groups clearly voted for him in recognition of his commitment to economic opportunity for all. In other words affirmative action was seen by many to be patronising, unfair and socially disruptive. They wanted someone who would improve the economic welfare of all Americans, including them, not simply someone who would preference their colour.

Even California, the most reliably Democrat state in the nation, delivered a stinging referendum rebuke to those wanting to restore affirmative action programs for minorities. This is particularly significant as California now has many more Hispanics and Asians than a decade ago when such affirmative action programs were fashionable.

Yet the 2020 referendum was lost by a double digit margin, despite a massive state-based campaign and huge financial resources being thrown at it. The majority clearly had come to the conclusion that such programs were not only socially divisive but deeply unfair to other non-privileged groups. They simply wanted a level playing field for all, in the best American tradition.

The best case study on race politics in support of this analysis was identified by Gerard Baker in *The Times* as Zapata County, Texas. With a population 85% Hispanic it had been solidly Democrat for the past 30 years. Hillary Clinton won it four years ago with almost two-thirds of the vote, yet in 2020 a majority of its voters went for Trump. This should be a wake up call for all race-focused progressives. Clearly these voters, like many millions of other Americans, realised that good policy outcomes and traditional values were more important than character per se and the constant disdain of the cultural elites.

The founding fathers were well aware that populists might emerge and threaten to derail democracy. As Anne Applebaum points out in *The Twilight of Democracy*, "Alexander Hamilton was so concerned to ensure that those with 'talents for low intrigue and the little arts of popularity' could never become President that he wanted the Electoral College to consist of elite lawmakers and men of property with the power to reject the people's choice if necessary, in order to avoid 'the excesses of democracy.'"

Fortunately, this extreme proposal was not adopted but, as a result of such concerns, the United States Constitution is riddled with checks and balances which impose serious limitations on potential freelancers. Despite the sound and fury which surrounded Donald Trump, he posed no lasting dangers to the democratic model.

The real issue from four years of Donald Trump is not whether you liked him or loathed him, but what he did in his term of office. Did he make America a safer and more prosperous country where all could aspire to succeed? Did he deliver on his promises?

Did he bring about a material improvement in the lives of those struggling to make ends meet – not necessarily those at the bottom of the pile but those hard-working strivers who are the backbone of the country, who worry about jobs, incomes and families and do not lie awake at night seething about gender diversity, identity issues or cancel culture? These were the very issues which brought Hillary Clinton undone while she was busy alienating ordinary hard-working Americans, with her odious "basket of deplorables" put down.

In a single term he achieved much more than Obama, George W. Bush and others in two terms and may well come to be regarded as the most successful of those eleven presidents who only served one term.

The significance of Trump's time in politics is not quantity but quality. It is much more about how he was able to diagnose America's decline and seize the moment to get America back on track. It was not about the theatre of politics, on which he thrived, but rather about addressing the root causes of the long-standing economic and cultural malaise which had befallen the country. It is truly extraordinary that no one else recognised that this was a once in a lifetime political market opportunity.

In some ways it was democracy's finest hour. The system was able to respond to the needs of the majority, press the reset button and change course – the political analogue of Schumpeter's "creative destruction". Finally, the American people had a politician who knew what had to be done to revitalise middle America and give its citizens hope for the future.

His genius was to discern what no one else understood – that the political establishment and its acolytes had gone off the rails and were much more interested in media-driven priorities such as gender equality, diversity, and identity politics than bread-and-butter issues of jobs and income.

The longer term issue is whether his focus on the middle class will survive him or whether career politicians will retreat to their comfort zones. He has shown the pathway to electoral success but will it be enough to maintain the momentum?

If his time in office serves as a wake-up call for the political class to cater more effectively for those in the middle ground, then America will have taken a giant step towards reinventing itself and thereby prolonging its pre-eminence as the leading nation in the world.

2

Trump in the White House

In the lead-up to the 2016 presidential election, Hillary Clinton, believing herself to be cruising to victory, made no serious attempt to address economic issues, preferring to play inside her comfort zone on gender and equality issues. Her "deplorables" fiasco was symptomatic of someone, serenely out of touch, who thought her issues were the only issues.

But, even after Trump's come-from-nowhere election victory, the Democrats seemed to think it was going to be business as usual. Or at least San Francisco uber liberal, Nancy Pelosi, did. Ahead of Trump's historic tax cuts of December 2017, the most extensive rewrite of the tax code in three decades, Pelosi, then Minority Leader in the House of Representatives, damned the plan as brazen theft, unrepentant greed and a moral obscenity – no way those robber barons would pass on the benefits to anyone but themselves and their shareholders. The GOP tax scam was not a vote for investment in growth or jobs, but a vote to install a permanent plutocracy in the nation.

How hysterical can you get – more importantly, how wrong can you get? This shrill and divisive rhetoric was proven wrong within days, as company after company promised to give their workers significant wage increases. In response to Trump's masterstroke of offering a one-off 15% tax on offshore earnings, around one hundred companies quickly announced major employee bonuses, wage increases and charitable donations.

Apple confirmed that it would repatriate most of the $US274

billion it held offshore, add 20,000 new jobs to its American workforce and establish a US$5 billion advanced manufacturing fund. Others, such as Microsoft, Pfizer, GE, Google and Cisco quickly followed suit, repatriating in all some $3 trillion in offshore reserves, roughly equivalent to Canada's entire GDP.

The stimulatory effect on the US economy was transformative, maybe even greater than the centrepiece of the plan. The dramatic cut in the corporate rate, from 35% to 21%, reverberated around the world. Obama had supported cutting the corporate rate a few years back, but back-flipped when it became politically convenient to say the opposite. The trouble with much partisan commentary was the indolent resort to the old extrapolation trick – look how much revenue will be lost – while completely ignoring the stimulus effect on the economy, via proactive responses of many major commercial participants.

The once great *Economist* has been a classic case in point. It could not bring itself to offer any in-depth analysis, contenting itself with a lazy grumble about the lack of experience available to the President and dismissing the Trump tax reforms as little more than a handout to companies and wealthy Americans. It complained about the increase in public borrowing (fair comment) but made no mention of the potentially stimulatory effect of the repatriation tax, and the likely massive inflow of funds to kick-start advanced manufacturing and the economy in general. The economy responded with vigour.

In the four years following Trump's unexpected victory the fury of his critics continued unabated. They were determined to deny him legitimacy and played every card with that object in mind. But they soon found out that he thrived on the assaults.

Trump Derangement Syndrome reached such levels because the Democrats became aware that many of his initiatives had found favour with the populace, so they were desperate to change the subject by impugning his integrity at every turn. First, they remorselessly pursued him for allegedly colluding with Russia, and when that fell flat they engaged in shameful mud-throwing over the nomination of Brett Kavanaugh for appointment to the Supreme Court, until he was finally confirmed by the Senate in October 2018.

Ultimately, in April 2019, the report of former FBI Director, Robert Mueller, effectively exonerated Trump of collusion with Russia. But by then the Democrats were in hot pursuit on the Biden-Ukraine front.

They even found it necessary to resort to the nuclear option of impeachment – the most dramatic in a series of failed attempts to hound him from office, on one of the weakest charge sheets of all time.

Although the Department of Justice had already cleared Trump of wrongdoing in relation to his call to the President of the Ukraine, this did not deter the Democrats from ploughing ahead with impeachment proceedings. These were justified by Nancy Pelosi, the new Speaker of the House of Representatives, as a necessary move to control a president who "has tried to make lawlessness a virtue in America and is now exporting it abroad."

Pelosi seemed to think that purple rhetoric would suffice, when history clearly shows that a smoking gun, not a popgun, is needed for successful impeachment.

As the *Wall Street Journal* categorically stated, there was simply no evidence that Trump had engaged in a quid pro quo by withholding aid to Ukraine, unless it "opened an investigation" into former Vice-President Joe Biden, even then a leading contender for the Democrat nomination for president in 2020.

Devastatingly, the Ukrainians said they had no knowledge the aid was being withheld until a month after the phone call. Trump's detractors did not seem to care that successful impeachment of a president is almost impossible without the commission of a patent "high crime" or "misdemeanour".

Nothing remotely of this ilk emerged and it was always unlikely that Republican members of Congress would desert Trump, any more than the Democrats had deserted Bill Clinton in his hour of need back in the late 1990s. The public remained totally unmoved and, with the unconvincing exception of Senator Mitt Romney of Utah, no Republican in either house was prepared to offer support. The attempt soon went down to ignominious defeat in the Senate.

That Trump was still standing bolt upright by 2020, notwithstanding contracting coronavirus, demonstrated not only his emotional resilience but the structural strength of America's distinctive system of checks and balances.

What is most extraordinary about the impeachment charade is that most media were frantically endeavouring to create a stench around the issue when Joe Biden seemed to be much more exposed and vulnerable than Trump. The whole world, including Joe Biden, knew that his son received $50,000 a month for being on the board of an energy company, notwithstanding that he had no expertise in the field, at the same time that his father was Vice-President of the United States.

Biden's defence tactic was to change the subject – it was an unconvincing strategy. He then tried stalling, later refusing to deny allegations of sexual impropriety until criticism from his own side forced him to respond publicly.

This particular political imbroglio is yet more evidence of Trump's diehard critics refusing to accept the legitimacy of his election and, by extension, the decision of the American people who elected him by due constitutional process. They seemed not to want to admit that the seeds of his triumph and Hillary Clinton's defeat lay in the creeping atrophy of politics as it had come to be practised in recent decades.

It had become an elite, self-absorbed game practised by insiders, indulging their pet projects and pandering to their support bases amidst the studied neglect of those less fortunate than themselves – middle America in general and the less educated, struggle-street inhabitants who suffer most from the purists' reckless pursuit of market freedoms, free trade and globalisation, without a second thought for its knock-on consequences and its impact on myriad displaced American workers.

These might all be worthy policy objectives for the greater national good, but they are often very bad news for the millions left behind. The result does not have to be autarchy and mercantilism. The response should, instead, take the form of serious endeavours to ameliorate the damage that often flows to those less able to sustain the blows.

In the 2018 mid-term elections Americans did not reject Trump – they only confirmed how durable his working class, rural, non-college educated coalition was. Long resisted by the Republican establishment, Trump effectively took over the Party, of which he had never hitherto been a member. Moderate suburban Republicans found themselves on the outer, along with the Never Trumpers. Ahead of the 2018 mid-term elections, Trump crossed America like a whirling dervish, as he was to do two years later. Wherever he went the crowds loved him.

Along the way he recast conservatism, recruiting many to his trade policies and tough line on immigration. Some Republican insiders were willing to take him on in the beginning, but they made no progress and quickly fell into line.

Trump was able to capitalise on an increasing sense among many conservative American citizens that the country was being led by people who did not share their views on matters such as illegal immigration, law and order, and traditional American values.

His mid-term pitch was again highly unorthodox. Instead of campaigning primarily on the unusually strong US economy, Trump chose to focus on social issues, particularly illegal immigration, playing to his base and ensuring that they would turn out the vote. It became clear then, and was subsequently confirmed in 2020, that his brand of nationalistic populism is unlikely to pass quickly – it is highly likely to outlast its creator and reconfigure US politics for a generation.

In 2016 Trump was elected by more than 63 million people who answered his call to overthrow the current political class, which for eight long years had consistently ignored his constituency. He was energised when pop star Madonna said she dreamed of blowing up the White House and Democratic Governor of New York, Andrew Cuomo, commented sourly, "America was never that great".

Most ordinary Americans did not see anything inherently evil in the idea of an American president putting America first, yet the very slogan provoked paroxysms of outrage amongst the left. It has been said that political liberalism has evolved over nearly three centuries from a philosophy of safeguarding freedoms into a philosophy of demanding rights.

Salvatore Babones, an American social scientist based in Sydney, has identified the new authoritarianism: "The greatest spiritual danger facing 21st century democracy is that liberal intellectuals increasingly dismiss the moral right of less educated people to have opinions that conflict with the consensus wisdom of the expert class". Liberal intellectuals completely ignore the fact that Britain, in 19th and early 20th centuries, went to the barricades to achieve universal suffrage. Now they want to take it away.

Famed Pulitzer Prize-winning columnist, the late Charles Krauthammer, said, as long ago as 2002, "To understand the workings of American politics you have to understand this fundamental law: Conservatives think liberals are stupid. Liberals think conservatives are evil". Such indulgent, inside-the-beltway self-loathing is a million miles removed from aspirational middle class America.

Professor David Gelernter, a computer scientist at Yale, wrote in October 2018:

Mr. Trump lacks constraints because he is filthy rich and always has been but, unlike other rich men, he revels in wealth and feels no need to apologise – ever. He never learned to keep his real opinions to himself because he never had to. He never learned to be embarrassed that he is male with ordinary male proclivities. Sometimes he has treated women disgracefully, for which Americans, left and right, are ashamed of him – as they are of JFK and Bill Clinton. I am sorry about the coarseness of the unconstrained average American that Mr. Trump conveys. But my job as a voter is to choose the candidate who will do best for America.

Trump's nasty name-calling was, at most times, quite counter-productive and calculated to make negotiating more difficult. But it is not always appreciated that, far from being anger-fuelled throwaways, the President's twittering and often inflammatory oral rhetoric was quite deliberately part of a narrative and a negotiating tool, which, in a number of instances, proved to be very effective.

He clearly reshaped how politics is conducted – at least for his term of office. The real issue, and the test of his legacy, will be whether Trump has permanently reshaped the manner and content of political debates so that the contest becomes much more focused on the lives, interests and aspirations of mainstream Americans.

As with Margaret Thatcher, so with Trump – the times can maketh the person. Thatcher came to office in the wake of a "winter of discontent" – endemic strikes, many working only a two-day week, rubbish piling up in the streets, the country out of control, the people begging for action. She had to restore "the sick man of Europe".

Trump had to re-start the engines of growth and rescue the leader of the free world from its malaise. Thatcher saw the need to restructure the economy and Britain's industrial framework. Trump saw the need to make the economy more accommodating to the needs of the masses. In doing so, he capitalised on the longings of the silent majority, many feeling an intense but unspoken hostility to the status quo.

The key to sustained national success is effective and continuing economic reform. Permanently constricting international trade will almost certainly impede US growth, certainly in the short-term, even if it is too early to assess offsetting benefits, predictable and unpredictable, of the historic tax package, especially the return of conventional and advanced manufacturing to America's shores.

The real problem addressed by Trump was not so much that domestic manufacturing had declined, but that employment in manufacturing had dropped from 17 million to 12 million, aided by automation and robotics, a trend very likely to continue.

This meant that real jobs growth, as usual, had to come from the small and medium-sized enterprises sector. It was his fervent hope that the combination of massive tax reductions, increased fuel production, deregulation of financial markets, the demise of environmental over-regulation and reduced compliance costs would make a big difference to America's competitiveness and economic efficiency.

Trump saw in the carbon reduction process clumsy, expensive, job-destroying interference and massive and unnecessary subsidies. He saw the future being driven much more by new technologies, responsive to immediate and growing market needs, and an environment which protected clean air and water and conservation of natural habitats.

There are certainly insights here for all policy-makers intent on re-engaging with mainstream voters. If the Biden administration, and particularly its leader, can acknowledge, even privately, that many of Trump's economic initiatives worked for the greater betterment, then they will be on the way to implementing a winning strategy.

As they say, good economics is usually good politics, but internal party political pressures from the ideological and the ambitious can blow a leader off course. The result is that leaders and parties are often more obsessed with product differentiation than with what works.

The big issue post-Trump will be the extent to which both parties have learned the crucial importance of middle America or whether politicians will fall back on their old ways and default to the rigid demands of their supporter base and their financial backers.

Trump realised that there are many who will never be persuaded, let alone won over, by positive economic news. He therefore needed to direct his primary appeals to the great unwashed, as conventional politics would only take him so far – better to create media bonfires, excite friends and foes alike and talk about criminal aliens and the wickedness of George Soros.

As Freddy Gray wrote in London's *The Spectator*:

> Trump is odious in many ways. But he's also a brilliant politician. He is brilliant because of, not despite, his odiousness. His monstrous ego keeps him going when the world says he is wrong, and voters admire him for that.

Trump frequently accused major news outlets of biased coverage and refused to engage with them. He preferred tweets and rallies because he did not trust the *New York Times*, the *Washington Post* or CNN to give him or his agenda a fair go. In fact, the bulk of the political press seemed to have decided that its role in life was to take down the Trump White House. In 2019 hundreds of newspapers nation-wide simultaneously published editorials attacking Trump in the guise of promoting a free press.

According to Democrat pollster Fred Yang: "The more Trump gets criticised by the media the more his base seems to rally behind him." It reached the stage where almost all self-identified

Republicans said they approved of the job he was doing, although the gap between Republican and Democrat views had never been wider.

Trump's core support group always combined those drawn to him for economic reasons as well as those drawn for cultural reasons. Particularly successful on questions of trade and immigration as far as white working class voters were concerned, the 2020 results will not give any comfort to the Democrats that his erstwhile supporters will waver on these critical issues.

The challenge for his successors will be to adopt what works, not what they would like to see happen.

3

Why Trump Lost

Donald Trump was a contrarian disruptor who was ultimately guilty of imperial overreach and became a vainglorious victim of his own success. His demise was largely the result of self-inflicted injuries, brought on by his unrelenting and largely unnecessary bombast.

He possessed considerable policy nous. It was his lack of political skills which ultimately brought him undone. Unlike four years ago when Hillary Clinton's toxicity was a winning factor for him, in 2020 he was up against a seemingly harmless and sometimes befuddled old man who had not offended anyone.

Because Trump could not resist the temptation to attack whenever possible – just part of his DNA – he neglected to run on his record, which was a substantial one. This allowed Biden, whose only campaign message seemed to be, "I'm not him", to make the pandemic and Trump's mishandling of it a key issue, instead of his own massive "tax and spend" proposals.

The media was also critically as helpful in turning the contest into a referendum on the character and personality of Trump, rather than a choice between competing offerings. Trump's achievements may have been well-known and appreciated but, in the fury of the campaign, they were swept aside in favour of a popularity contest.

But, while he lost the 2020 presidential election contest to Joe Biden, much that he stood for came through largely unscathed. As the UK *Telegraph*'s Charles Moore scoffed, "hardly a new dawn for the Left". There was no stunning repudiation of his presidency, as many commentators and other "experts" had confidently predicted. They must have been aghast that he won more than 48% of the popular vote and precipitated the highest voter turnout in history. Moreover, despite having a huge fund-raising advantage and almost unanimous media backing, the Democrats barely won the Senate and suffered significant losses in the House and state legislatures.

Biden's campaign advertisements were, no doubt deliberately, anodyne and largely biographical, contrasting his character with that of Trump. He barely mentioned the big-spending, left-leaning agenda he had agreed to under pressure from Bernie Sanders – perfectly legitimate, as campaign strategies go, but gifted a free pass by a media overwhelmingly willing him on. Oblivious to their professional responsibilities, they barely asked Biden any tough questions, especially regarding the multiple peccadillos of his errant son, Hunter.

Donald Trump was a product of his times. Only he, among the political class, had appreciated that mainstream America was crying out for serious structural reform and was sick to death of political correctness. He understood that the forgotten Americans were essentially voiceless in the public domain but would endorse any politician prepared to address the reality of their daily lives and needs. This he proceeded to do during his four years in office and was on track for a second term, until the coronavirus black swan appeared out of a clear blue sky and he was blown off course.

His critical failures – one of judgment, the other of tempera-ment – served to alienate a statistically significant proportion of previously rusted on supporters, who finally lost the faith. In a tight election he could ill afford to lose these defectors from his base of white working class voters. Eventually he sank under the weight of his own personal shortcomings.

Given his achievements in government and having honoured almost all his election promises, he should have been cruising to victory, virus or no virus. Trump's biggest mistake was to continue in government as he had behaved in opposition. Being such an irredeemable pugilist, he would rather have had a fight than a feed any day. But in office these habits of a lifetime became more of a liability.

None of his breakthrough policies needed to be accompanied by wild and, at times, highly irresponsible, rudeness and insults. This is where character, self-discipline and nuance come in. Any serious reflection should have shown him that he enjoyed widespread support for transforming the economy and, at least pre-Covid, the voters were grateful.

Neither a committed Republican nor a practising conservative, he had, by sheer force of personality, effectively imposed himself on the Republican Party. He was no ideologue and had little interest in history.

He was first and last a business entrepreneur who sought to apply a lifetime of business principles and practices to a craft of which he had little first-hand experience. Unlike nine of his predecessors, he was not a war hero and without any public office achievements; he had no stored political capital.

Moreover, his multitude of personal character failings made him a deeply polarising figure. Not only an amoralist but a true vulgarian, he did not hesitate to exaggerate or even fabricate in order to portray himself in the most positive light. As a result many found him deeply offensive and became "Never Trumpers", who were unable to bring themselves to look objectively at his performance in office.

He certainly displayed strong leadership but it was accompanied by an utter intolerance of his political enemies and a quickness to deride and even humiliate any opposing views. Government demands a degree of statesmanship and governing for all, while Opposition allows regular and targeted attacks, with florid rhetoric being generally acceptable.

Four years ago it had been Trump's good fortune to be up against a very weak and conceited opponent in Hillary Clinton, viscerally disliked by millions and solipsistically oblivious to the needs and concerns of middle America.

His moniker of "crooked Hillary" rang a loud bell for millions, disgusted by her constant dissembling. Biden, on the other hand, was much harder to nail. Old, weak, lazy, sleepy might have been accurate, but they were not devastating.

As it turned out, in 2016 Trump had been pushing against an open door. His lifelong familiarity with the working class, both as a businessman and a celebrity, had given him insights that no one else seems to have had – that millions of ordinary working class middle Americans were more than fed up with their everyday financial struggles being ignored and increasingly infuriated by Obama's preference for identity politics and Clinton's keenness to deliver more of same. But he would not have succeeded with a conventional political approach and without offering real and substantial policy changes.

The left of centre media and the Democrat Party tend largely to focus on the bottom income quartile in the mistaken belief that they will get credit, and votes, from the rest of society for their compassion and apparent empathy. But middle America is smarter than that – it knows that such an approach is not only likely to be very expensive but also unlikely to be very effective in growing the economy, and thereby generating the revenue and resources to deliver jobs, income and national prosperity.

Even four years earlier millions of Americans had found Trump's distasteful egotism impossible to ignore and were simply not interested in his promises, let alone his achievements. This was particularly the case with the elites, many of them residents of comfortable, middle class "mega-enclaves" in California, New

York and the District of Columbia. They saw themselves as superior intellectual and moral animals and detested his "bourgeois values".

Ultimately the perpetually outraged were outnumbered by those who had a better focus on bread and butter issues and wanted an economy that delivered national and family security. These were concerns which the elites could afford to take for granted; to the hard-pressed working class, these were life and death matters.

These included large swathes of non-tertiary educated, blue-collar workers and millions of women, many of whom probably held their noses whilst doing so but were prepared to vote for Trump for the real changes he offered.

It is hard to believe that his inept handling of coronavirus was fatal, although it does seem to be the case that around the world leaders who have handled this issue well have scored record high approval ratings. Even in Australia, state premiers who have for-saken the economic consequences and put the health issue front and centre, with more regard for the politics than the science, have done well in the popularity stakes. Trump was not one of those.

Whether or not he thought that the relentless aggression which had won him the Presidency would do the same again this time, it is hard to understand why he did not ask himself whether it was necessary, given its negative consequences. He would certainly not have been seen as a wimp if he had adopted a somewhat more moderate tone. When he did throw the switch to discipline at the 2020 Republican convention, and again in the second debate, he scored well.

The answer is probably that he became over-confident and simply could not help himself – he became a one trick pony who behaved like a cave man (not of the sentimental Fred Flintstone variety) and enjoyed the blood sport too much. His never-ending verbal aggression ultimately proved counter-productive and led to a significant breakaway movement of Trump defectors who had supported his policy initiatives but had become sick and tired of rhetorical indiscipline.

His press conferences, particularly in defence of his Covid actions, were often little more than meandering rants which did not persuade anyone. This indiscipline proved to be the difference between winning and losing. Leading foreign affairs commentator Greg Sheridan has described it as "failing to normalise his presidency".

In some ways the mere fact that he had accomplished a lot and improved the welfare of the majority meant that enough people felt they could bank these gains, take a breather and opt for someone for whom they had generally low expectations but not big apprehensions.

This electoral perversity is not an altogether uncommon phenomenon. Voters ultimately tired of long serving and successful prime ministers in John Howard (Australia, 2007), Stephen Harper (Canada, 2015) and John Key/Bill English (New Zealand, 2017).

Each of these leaders had governed well but ultimately their electorates seem to have formed the view that the economy was running on automatic pilot and could be safely entrusted to others.

In Trump's case the time span was much shortened, due to the non-stop dramas which bedevilled his term.

It is, however, extraordinary that not long before the election a Gallup poll had 56% of respondents saying they were better off than four years ago – significantly better than Barack Obama (45%) and George W. Bush (47%) at the same stage, and both of them were elected to second terms.

This indicates that voters did not hold Trump responsible for soaring post-Covid unemployment and very much approved of his economic stimulus program.

But to lose despite those numbers also shows the ultimately

lethal effectiveness of the constant guerrilla campaign waged by Pelosi, Schumer and others, who certainly never accepted the validity of the 2016 result. It is also an indictment of the way politics is now being played, especially if it encourages others to follow suit.

Trump's determination to dominate the media space and pound away relentlessly and indiscriminately at every conceivable target gave Biden the opportunity and, thanks to coronavirus, the excuse to become a small target.

Hiding under the doona in his Delaware man-cave for months on end would ordinarily have been regarded as not only politically counter-intuitive, but a likely career-ending strategy. In Biden's case it was a godsend, as it minimised his chances of "misspeaking" by coming up with more of his nonsensical non sequiturs which cast doubt not only on his mental acuity, but his likely longevity and, with it, the prospect of an extreme lurch to the left under a totally unproven Kamala Harris.

But while the default reaction to the result, particularly of the elites, may be to consider Trump a failure, this is likely to prove to be both a premature and an inaccurate assessment. He is now the eleventh president to be defeated when running for a second term, the third since World War II, the last nearly thirty years ago, but his many achievements stack up well against the best of them.

The reason why the lessons of history are important is that they ultimately deliver judgements on performance, from which we can learn what works and what does not. The supercharged emotions which can and do drive voting decisions fade away and the focus reverts to the scoreboard and not the crowd. Over time, reputations can change, sometimes quite dramatically. Ronald Reagan now enjoys a much better press than he did during his lifetime.

Harry Truman left office with the lowest approval ratings for an outgoing president, yet today is generally regarded as a successful leader. Historians generally rank Lincoln as America's most respected president yet in his time he was vilified and viewed with contempt by many. Ulysses S. Grant's two terms were mired in scandal and administrative shortcomings but he is now regarded as one of the best.

In the modern era JFK's reputation has been sullied by his rampant infidelities. The true believers in Camelot still treat him as a god-like progressive, but historians are increasingly categorising him as both a social and fiscal conservative.

He liked and admired Nixon and their friendship continued throughout JFK's life. For nearly fifty years Richard Nixon has been the quintessential bad guy, being the only president to resign in disgrace. In 1993, while Bill Clinton was in office, Nixon sent him a report on Russia which Clinton described as "the most brilliant communication on foreign policy" to reach him as president. Years later, in delivering a eulogy at Nixon's funeral, he said: "May the day of judging President Nixon on anything less than his entire life and career come to a close".

Yet, while these more mature judgments may bring post facto solace to their admirers, the fact remains that to lose the confidence of a sufficient numbers of voters is to lose office. Clearly, for all his heroics, Trump suffered an ultimately fatal voter drift which has to be attributed to the character and behaviour of the individual and not to what he achieved.

In many respects he threw the presidency away. In fact history may decide that there were two Trumps – one very successful in both the domestic and international policy arenas, the other an outlandish boor whose behaviour was so outrageous as to deem him unsuitable to hold the highest office.

Ultimately his fatal lack of insight was little more than self-indulgence. His base had voted for him in the hope that he would be a change agent and, given that his term in office was very much about the things they wanted, they could have been expected to vote for him again on the same basis.

None of his breakthrough policies needed to be accompanied by wild and at times highly irresponsible rudeness and insults. This is where character and self-discipline come in. Any serious reflection should have shown Trump that he had transformed the economy and, at least pre-Covid, the voters were grateful.

The Trump experiment should demonstrate conclusively that nearly all elections are about the hip pocket nerve. He won the 2016 election because he addressed the issues that were important to millions of working Americans: jobs, tax cuts, immigration, economic and national security. These were the equivalent of Morrison's quiet Australians. Unfortunately for Trump, although his policy instincts were very much in tune with his rusted-on constituency, his volatile and, at times, inexcusable behaviour ended up costing him very dearly.

Thus Trump may well go down in history as one of the very few successful one term presidents, maybe even the best.

The general operating principle for both sides of politics has, for many years, been to cater for special interest groups. In the case of the Democrats, this means groups such as unions and minorities and, for the Republicans, big business and large donors. In addition there are often wealthy individuals with a cause to pursue.

Yet a series of elections around the world in recent years should by now have demonstrated that the single largest bloc which can decide elections is the middle income working class. And it was this group that Trump rode to victory in 2016. If his Republican successors can bring themselves to adopt his winning formula, then his legacy will be a long lasting one.

The question of character

If you believe some academic progressives, character is all in politics. According to the director of Oxford University's Centre for Corporate Reputation: "The research is pretty clear ... it's character that matters much more than capability when it comes to politics". This analysis was proffered, in sorrow, to explain why Hillary Clinton, "an incredibly capable woman", lost in 2016. The obvious rejoinder that people therefore clearly preferred the character of Donald Trump was ignored.

I do not think that even his most fervent supporters would argue that, but it is a nice illustration of the ends to which some diehard Trump haters will go to avoid the obvious conclusion – that the majority clearly preferred what Trump had to offer. It also ignores what capabilities were in question, as Trump had an abundance of real life business, commercial and practical experience, whereas Clinton's career record was completely confined to playing the political game. But whether Trump runs again or not, his passionate cult following is not going away, and middle Americans will continue to be a force to be reckoned with.

Oceans of words have already been written and spoken about Trump's unique basket of unattractive personality shortcomings and their significance. But perhaps the best, and ultimately one of the most constructive, assessments has come from the pen of Joseph Epstein, the doyen of political observers, who has seen it all.

He correctly observed that Trump's rebarbative personality had served to negate his many accomplishments: "Almost daily he demonstrated he was devoid of graciousness … he revealed a taste for insult, an unrelenting boastfulness and arrogance, and a general coarseness", which ultimately became too much for even the more refined who recognised what he had done to turn the country, and its culture, around.

But Epstein also paints a vivid picture of what the mainstream found so outrageous: American cities taken over by rioters and looters claiming they were protesting about "systemic racism", students denying others the right to speak and then claiming they felt unsafe even behind ivy-covered walls – and all this condoned and even encouraged by a weak and compliant media, only interested in fomenting controversy and civil unrest in order to promote their commercial interests, as well as their own "progressive" instincts.

Why should not middle Americans accept that Trump's relentlessly boorish behaviour was a price worth paying for an end to madness and a return to more traditional values? They did not vote for a choirboy; they wanted a serious change agent – and they got one, in spades!

It should also be stressed that an understandable personal antipathy was magnified to gargantuan proportions by an out-of-control media, which from the outset abandoned any trace of objectivity and declared total war on someone they loathed – his wealthy upbringing, his raw capitalist spirit, his uncultivated manner, his mockery of political correctness and his unwillingness to accept their unrelenting bias against him. Second time around it can be said that the left media got their man, but not really – he got himself.

4

America's Forgotten People

Why "the deplorables" matter

Most Australian travellers to the United States make obligatory visits to New York City, Washington, DC, Chicago and Los Angeles, with few deviations. I had been no exception. Although I had travelled extensively through New England, upstate and downstate New York, and California, as well as having enjoyed an extensive drive through the Deep South, with side trips to Arizona and Texas, my experience of travelling through middle America had been largely confined to driving between New York and Washington, on several occasions.

The unique opportunity to visit Ohio for the 2016 Republican Convention was an opportunity to have a good look at Pennsylvania, Indiana and Michigan, before reaching Cleveland, Ohio, on the southern shore of Lake Erie. It was a revelation to see the ravages of rust belt decline in once prosperous cities like Detroit, but there were also some green shoots.

I managed to spend some time in the Amish community around Holmes County, Ohio, the second largest aggregation of one of the last bastions of cultural conservatism outside Lancaster County, Pennsylvania, which I had visited a few years earlier. These hard working and morally upright people do not normally vote but they were certainly not out of place in the mid-west.

The contrast between ordinary working people, who voted solidly for Trump less than six months later, and the highly urban communities in New York, the District of Columbia, and California, which delivered huge majorities for Clinton, could not have been greater.

The information impact on these prosperous locations, where the most prestigious print and television media (the *New York Times*, the *Washington Post*, CNN and CBS), replete with their traditional soft left bias, are based, has only recently been offset by the arrival of a conservative newcomer, Fox News.

Their hallowed pedigrees notwithstanding, these left wing media stalwarts comprehensively missed the election result – just like Australia's ABC, whose reporters mostly live in comfortable urban surrounds, rarely coming into contact with ordinary Australians, whom they assume think like them – how could any right-thinking person not do so? Or, alternatively, they believe ordinary Australians, or, at least, their viewers, are simply in desperate need of endless drip-feeds of compassion and moralism.

The concept of the "forgotten man" has a long and controversial history in American politics. Over the years the term has undergone subtle variations in meaning. In today's world, even the nomenclature has changed, with "the forgotten people" better reflecting gender equality awareness.

The 19th century Yale sociologist, William Graham Sumner, is often credited was coining the original term and exploring its implications. In a famous 1883 political essay he lamented the lost autonomy of hard-working citizens forced to pay for high-flown programs of social reform. Andrew Jackson, a serial disruptor of an earlier age, had talked in terms of "the bone and sinew of the country", but the concept had not yet matured.

In 1932, in the depths of the Great Depression, Franklin Roosevelt invoked "the forgotten man" to represent factory workers and struggling farmers – ordinary citizens without whom a modern economy would falter. But his solution was government prescriptions – a legal minimum wage, legislated Social Security protections and a mandated federal right to organise unions.

But gradually the concept became a term of abuse to describe a change-resistant, redneck lower middle class. It became alien to the thinking of the "progressive" elites, who refused to recognise the real grievances and desires of what had once been a bedrock Democrat constituency.

In the mid-20th century, the support of Australia's longest serving prime minister, Robert Menzies, for "lifters rather than leaners", was another doffing of the political cap to those engaged in physical labour, and his continued advocacy on behalf of "the forgotten people" became a constant in the Australian political dialogue.

Australian voters at the 2019 Federal election will be very familiar with the Morrison variation of "the quiet Australians". And the same cohort had a key role to play in the 2015 English election and the Brexit referendum.

In contrast to the earlier big government solutions, Trump, from a highly competitive commercial background, was more concerned to reinvigorate the sluggish free enterprise economy by removing the shackles of overregulation.

His concerns were immediately greeted with the usual disparagements from the progressives and the elites, as well as the majority of media commentators, the term, "populist", quickly becoming the put down *du jour*.

Whereas Roosevelt and his ideological successors thought in terms of the white working class man, Trump's vision was much broader. His pitch covered all lower paid hard-working Americans, male or female, irrespective of colour. He wanted solutions that would raise wages, and not merely incomes for all workers, regardless of educational attainment. His critics liked to frame the debate in terms of race and class; Trump was more interested in earnings levels.

He understood the preoccupation of macroeconomists with the benefits of free trade, which boosted the national economy, but he was also acutely conscious that the gains largely went to the already wealthy and often jeopardised the livelihoods of those in lower paid, unskilled jobs. Trade agreements like the Trans-Pacific Partnership, although likely to boost GDP, threatened to make the possibility of secure middle-class jobs even more elusive for non-college educated workers.

Trump also well understood that big business would always seek to relocate manufacturing activities to lower cost economies but he was impatient with the often disingenuous liberal solution of "retraining" as he knew that older, unskilled workers were most unlikely to be able to seamlessly adapt to new skilled work requirements. Already a large proportion of older US males were out of work with no serious prospects of job re-entry and he did not wish to add more to the scrapheap.

The Global Financial Crisis had hit the lower working classes hard, and not just in financial terms. They watched with fury as big banks were bailed out, while they were sold out. By 2016 the continued neglect of their concerns had reached boiling point, but few in the public forums realised it.

A *Reuters* 2016 exit poll found that 75% of respondents agreed that: "America needs a strong leader to take the country back from the rich and powerful", and after eight years of insipid economic leadership by Barack Obama and the promise of more of same by Hillary Clinton, a close friend of the "rich and powerful", middle America had had enough.

The poll also showed that 68% believed that "traditional parties and politicians do not care about people like me". This played straight into the hands of Donald Trump. They particularly resented talk show hosts, so-called "comedians" and media presenters who mocked them as illiterate bumpkins who could not find places like the Ukraine on the map. Obama's earlier characterisation of them as "bitter individuals, clinging to guns and religion", still rankled and Hillary Clinton's "deplorables" slur was the last straw.

While the rank and file and "Never Trumpers" inside the Republican Party vented their displeasure with him in public, they little realised that they were simply reinforcing voter support for Trump as the ultimate outsider, with no serious adherence to either major party. To him, as with Bernie Sanders in the Democrat Party, membership of the Republican Party was merely a flag of convenience.

It is also probably true to say that pundits and pollsters fundamentally failed to appreciate the intense, reality-distorting power of Trump's long-standing national fame. There was an unwillingness to believe that people of colour would not instinctively reject him because of unseemly "racist" comments when, like many women, they were more concerned to support someone who offered them hope and a path out of misery.

While some in the media liked to claim that Trump's "forgotten Americans" were just disaffected, angry, white voters, Trump always made it clear that his policies were designed to create jobs and lower taxes for all and to open up opportunities which helped everyone, including blacks and other minorities and, in large measure, they did.

Wages for typical workers, particularly in the construction and manufacturing sectors, had been stagnating for more than thirty-five years. Almost two-thirds of those in the workforce (65.1%) – a majority in every state – did not have a college degree.

But, thanks to his repeal of hundreds of job-killing restrictions and regulations, the pre-Covid economy grew at record rates and unemployment fell to levels not seen in fifty years, with women, minorities and other lowest-income earners amongst the greatest beneficiaries. Moreover, increased energy production lowered fuel and heating costs – very important matters for lower income workers.

Within a few years the political impact was becoming clear to more astute observers, such as former Obama adviser and CNN commentator Van Jones, who warned early in 2020 that African-Americans were starting to gravitate to the then president because he had delivered results for them. And he was not talking about results on racial issues – these "forgotten people", like most Americans, simply wanted economic progress; they saw themselves as part of the mainstream, not a separate class or group, as liberal commentators liked to pretend.

The same could also be said for Latinos, 32% of whom voted for Trump, and an increasing proportion of Asian Americans. Cuban and Venezuelan voters also were primarily concerned with economic issues, having been badly hurt by a socialist straight-jacket previously imposed on them.

Although there are a number of discrete policies and value statements which make up a political persona, ultimately it is the candidate's overall position on the spectrum which is determinative for many voters. So, despite her efforts to portray herself as merely "a progressive", most still regarded Hillary Clinton as a hard-core liberal.

Nearly 18 months before the 2016 presidential election, 538, the polling website run by Nate Silver, had conducted a review of multiple analyses and found that she was seen as slightly more liberal than Barack Obama and barely more moderate than Bernie Sanders. In the two years they shared in the Senate, they had voted the same way 93% of the time.

Given that the elites still seem to have a very jaundiced view of the lower classes and progressive Democrats are not far behind, it is worthwhile looking at a very important essay to see the extent to which the Hillary Clinton's agenda resonated with mainstream America.

Isabel Sawhill is an economist and senior fellow at the Brookings Institution. She is also a life-long Democrat and a former Clinton administration official. In 2018 she published *The Forgotten Americans: An Economic Agenda for a Divided Nation*, based on a two-year study of those left behind, many of whom self-identified as "lower middle class" or "working class" and voted for Donald Trump. The Forgotten Americans constitute 38% of the working age population, are in the bottom half by family income distribution, and lack a college degree.

One of her key findings was that hard working Americans do not have the time or inclination to study policy detail but they do want government solutions that reflect their values and priorities: education, work and family, but especially work. "I heard over and over that people want to be self-supporting. Above all, they want decent jobs. They believe they are responsible for what happens to them and rarely blame 'the system' or outside forces for their plight".

Most understood the need for "a bit of self-discipline" and disliked freeloading. She quoted a 51-year-old draftsman from Syracuse, whom, she said, captured many participants' views when he said: "I don't think it's the government's responsibility to take care of people".

They were also wary of the need for higher taxes, an old Democrat favourite, and many respondents preferred cutting programs or government outlays that they did not like. Moreover, quite a few resisted the idea that anyone needed to pay more, even those on higher incomes, who had mostly worked hard for it.

Her assessment was that "[l]iberal elites who think we can redistribute income between rich and poor do not understand the definition of fairness that most Americans hold: 'if you earned it, no matter the amount, you should get to keep it' ". No doubt many are aspirational, hoping to be get their own just rewards one day.

She also identified the narrative that rose to the top and was, she considered, too important to ignore: "Some Americans are disgusted with how government has been working (or, more, accurately, not working) and they want change – any change". Sounds like they were just praying for Donald Trump to come along.

She concluded: "My main message to liberals is that a new set of big and expensive government programs may appeal to liberal elites and political activists but will not appeal to the average voter."

These are breathtaking findings. When I first read them they sounded like a straight lift from a right of centre manifesto. They undermine the dominant Democrat (and Australian Labor) Party world view and an ethos which is overwhelmingly predicated on government both finding and funding the solutions, via ever more handouts, increased welfare entitlements and special schemes. They also put the lie to the irresistible inclination of most media to parse the electorate by race and class. Her findings make it clear that many, if not most, middle class ethnic groups think along the same lines as their white compatriots, with mainstream attitudes to divisive issues. But because there will always be racial activists, from Barack Obama down, aided and abetted by many media keen to fan the flames, the polarisation continues.

The "poor white trash", whom Clinton so deplored, could also be described as hard-working, tax-paying Americans, and proud of it. As Isabel Sawhill makes clear, they were not the poor, unemployed welfare class, so beloved of the Democrats, at least in gesture.

They were the middle 50% of Americans, best defined as "the working class", not looking for sympathy or for moral support, but for real and lasting job opportunities to support themselves and their families. They also put a high value on self-reliance and personal responsibility.

A leading left wing academic, Professor Joan Williams, has explained that the alleged horror of "right wing populism" is largely to be attributed to decades of condescension and "class cluelessness", by which she means a lack of appreciation by the left political class that those who supported Trump were not the poorest at the bottom of the ladder. They were the mass of ordinary hard-working families.

This is where elections are won and lost. The media, ever looking for novelty, usually prefers to focus on the misfortunes of slivers of society. Meanwhile, left-of-centre parties and their supporters fool themselves that the mainstream will welcome this moral concern for others when, like almost everyone else, they put themselves first.

None of this is to suggest that most people are indifferent to the sufferings of others, simply that they resent being told that this is the main game, as the constant preachings of the Greens and their media soulmates like to suggest.

Team Clinton was oblivious to the real concerns of this huge cohort, even though it had the power to make or break her, as it did. The Labor Party in Australia under Bill Shorten, desperate to be different, fell into the same trap. The 2019 Federal Election, yet again, proved that the Australian middle class, perhaps the largest per capita segment in the world, are not interested in class warfare or anti-business rhetoric.

Most are very keen on gainful employment, many running their own small businesses, and are not at all attracted to living off government handouts.

When I try to analyse why the Democrats and other left-of-centre parties completely miss what the voting middle class really want, my conclusion is this: Politicians, actual and potential, pore over every word in the newspapers and take note of every political comment on television and online, not just because they are political junkies, which they are, but also because it is easier than trying to find things out for yourself. They cannot take the temperature of every relevant voter so they treat the zeitgeist as a simulacrum for community thinking which must be listened to, accommodated, and responded to as sympathetically as possible.

They believe that the media can make or break a political career so it must not be offended. The media's agenda and commercial imperative are political excitement, colour and movement, which is the very opposite of how we live our lives, but it pretends that it is only upholding the national interest and offering constructive advice, which can change whenever the occasion demands. This reminds me of Groucho Marx: "Those are my principles, and if you don't like them … well, I have others".

As the media are predominantly left wing and everyone is an expert on social policy, it is much easier to generate screaming headlines based on a single example of aberrant behaviour or the foibles of human nature than to focus on a boring economics analysis. Those who regard social issues as more important, even more moral or virtuous, than economic ones, will readily take their steer from a media outlet which caters for them.

The media are expert at tugging at our heartstrings, with endless stories about the poor, the homeless, drug victims, refugees, prisoners, the blind, the crippled, the lame and the mentally afflicted. The list is virtually endless and it is not hard to imply that all of the above are deserving of our help and support and always that the government is not doing, or spending, enough to alleviate the problem.

As a result, parties like the Democrats are encouraged to not only believe that poverty alleviation is the main game but that government must do everything in its power to improve society's lot, virtually irrespective of the expense, let alone who pays for it and how.

So the principal target of their policies tends to be the bottom level of society, whom they regard as more in need and therefore more deserving of government largesse, and hopefully delivering sufficient media applause to get them over the line at election time. This approach may be admirable in a moral sense but ignores the reality that governments have to balance a multitude of competing interests, all of whom have the right to vote. And if political parties want to be on the winning side and able to implement their favoured policies, they have to take a hard-nosed, realist approach.

The Forgotten American's priorities make a mockery of those of Hillary Clinton: feminism, affirmative action, gender equality, sugar taxes, trans toilets. Working middle America was not interested in "daring to dream" about the first female president; they simply wanted one who would be there for them. In fact many of her priorities probably would not appeal to even the lowest decile, most of whom are not in gainful employment and are more likely to be principally concerned with poverty amelioration rather than poverty elimination, even if they turn their minds to such issues.

The ultimate conclusion therefore is that the Democrats have allowed the media to dictate their agenda in the mistaken belief that doing so will deliver an electoral reward. But, if one thing should already be crystal clear, it is that, with almost every mainstream media outlet irredeemably hostile to everything that Trump stood for, he managed to attract more that 74 million votes. In other words, it was the voters who made up their own minds and voted accordingly. That they were able to do so is a profound tribute to the health of American democracy, but also a timely reminder of the importance of the forgotten people.

5

Underestimating the Donald

Donald Trump's victory in 2016 must go down in the annals of American politics as one of the most masterful strategic achievements of all time. He went into what everyone expected to be another conventional campaign as a rank outsider. He never bothered to articulate his vision, but his research clearly told him what must have been hidden in clear sight to everyone else.

Working Americans, the backbone of the economy, had been ignored by conventional politicians for decades. They had had enough. But because they were ordinary hard-working individuals, with families and mortgages to support, they had neither the time nor the inclination to take to the streets or burst into print. Only Trump knew they were ripe for the picking. But it was his tactical *modus operandi* that had genius written all over it. Instead of swapping polite political phrases with his opponent, he declared war on her and what she stood for, and deliberately used inflammatory language to provoke the media and turn its reaction to his advantage.

Hillary Clinton's lavishly resourced campaign should also have identified these same strong undercurrents, but presumably Trump's nostrums were dismissed as politically untenable, as well as morally abhorrent. His superior reading of the tea leaves might seem a political masterstroke in hindsight but, at the time, it flew in the face of every conventional thinking person's idea of a winning strategy, and therefore constituted a huge leap into the unknown. But he was used to making high risk, high reward calls and would have lost little sleep using a clear and colourful, at times extreme, message to stand out from other candidates.

In Australia we like to think that product differentiation is very important, but we rarely think outside the box to the extent that Trump did. "Make America Great Again", a slogan recycled from the Reagan era, was a masterstroke which worked for Trump at multiple levels. Insiders baulked at its banality and unoriginality, while overlooking its almost irresistibly powerful message. As Trump did not rely on insiders, he did not make that mistake. Another priceless slogan was "drain the swamp", again, not original, but it attracted instant voter recognition and widespread approval. These were an advertising agency's dream lines, in this case valued in votes.

In passing, it is worth commenting that the Coalition's successful slogan at the 2019 Australian election was also a masterstroke, which pithily summed up all that was wrong with the Shorten package, "the Bill that Australia cannot afford", a simple, powerful and ultimately devastating riposte, yet roundly ignored by the media and analysts alike.

The way to preserve robust democracies like the United States and Australia is to ensure that economic policies are primarily geared towards the broad mass of people. This also helps to ensure that the concerns of those who are otherwise likely to be attracted to fringe parties, such as Pauline Hanson's One Nation, will largely be addressed.

Corporations and the affluent middle class can usually cope with whatever government throws at them. Poor and even average families are much more at risk. We must always be ready to come to the aid of the disadvantaged, but obsessive pandering to exotic minority interests is not the way to go. Everyone opposes bullying, but no one should stand passively by when it is used as an excuse to impose radical gender theory on the very young and impressionable.

Trump's promises

Most successful presidential candidates do their best to honour their campaign promises. Trump was no exception, despite sections of the press urging him to reneg, soften his language, be more polite. He continued to speak bombastically and twitter unmercifully. No one was in any doubt about his meaning – no weasel words, no political correctness, just plain words that everyone could understand.

Notwithstanding that his language was at times undoubtedly ugly, it was also incisive – as used to be said about my much-loved Queensland National Party Senate colleague, Ron Boswell, "not pretty, but pretty effective".

In politics, words can be bullets. Hillary Clinton had either not heard of this verity or had forgotten its truth. To tell a group of clean energy types, "We're going to put a lot of coal miners and coal companies out of business," was tantamount to telling workers in more than half a dozen coal producing states like Wyoming, West Virginia, Kentucky and Pennsylvania, "you're fired." Maybe this explains her reluctance to visit, let alone campaign in, some key states. But no-one can afford to write off a group of key states.

To make matters worse, only a month or so later she came out with the infamous, never to be forgotten, "basket of deplorables". Hardly the way to win friends and influence people, let alone voters.

These potentially fatal howlers emphasise the need for constant alertness and discipline, even in front of a friendly audience, where you might like to think that your remarks are "off the record." As we should all know by now, every word in an e-mail, every selfie or Instagram can find its way into the media, so "think first" is the golden rule. It applies above all to political leadership, where the stakes are highest.

Trump's qualifications

Donald Trump's path to the White House was more than unconventional – it was unique. He was no smooth talking Ivy League professional or military hero, but by the time of the 2016 election he was an established high achiever, having carved out successful careers in the two highly competitive industry sectors of construction and entertainment.

Trump, the showman with a nationwide following, had the perfect persona to launch a people-based movement. Just as Andrew Jackson had broken away from the founding fathers, so Donald Trump sought to do the same from the post-war establishment.

After eight years of so-called progressive politics under the Democratic regime of Barack Obama, millions of Americans were clearly thirsting for something, almost anything, else. Obama might have been a great orator; for many that was enough. A product of the Democrats' increasing obsession with identity politics, he filled their bill as the first African-American president.

Scant attention was given to his qualifications for the presidency. After graduating from Columbia University in 1983, he worked as a community organiser in Chicago. In 1988 he enrolled in Harvard Law School, where he was the first black person to be president of the *Harvard Law Review*.

After graduation, he became a civil rights attorney and an academic, teaching constitutional law at the University of Chicago Law School from 1992 to 2004. He then spent ten years in elective politics, first as an Illinois state senator (1997-2004), then as a United States senator for Illinois (2005-08).

None of this reeks of any substantial achievements other than climbing the greasy political pole. Essentially he remained a political dilettante with undergraduate instincts – not interested in negotiating across the aisle, rarely reaching out to his own side, more interested in scoring rhetorical points, basically from the Jimmy Carter school of "lead from behind" diplomacy.

He was ashamed of capitalism, embarrassed by American exceptionalism and held a normative view of the world, much more of an idealist than a realist, who preferred "feel good" dialogue to serious economic debate any day. After eight non-productive years middle America was thoroughly fed up with a declining economy and being ignored when not being spoken down to.

They had no empathy for Obama's obsession with identity politics. In the lead up to his successful 2008 campaign, Obama had revealed his true thoughts about working class voters in old industrial towns decimated by job losses: "They get bitter, they cling to guns or religion or antipathy to people who are not like them or anti-immigrant sentiment or anti-trade sentiment as a way to explain their frustrations."

Obama's strident put down of religion was later magnified by his vindictive attempt to force the nuns of the Little Sisters of the Poor to dispense contraceptives in violation of their central religious beliefs. His clear distaste for conventional religion provided Trump with a golden opportunity and he, hardly a religious person, hoovered up support from the religious communities. Early in 2019 Trump's Administration reversed Obama's political oppression.

In a few sentences Obama had shown his distaste for millions of hard-working middle Americans – and they never forgot. Hillary Clinton, then competing with Obama for the Democratic nomination, had quickly seen the devastating potency of his remarks: "I was taken aback by the demeaning remarks Senator Obama made about people in small town America. His remarks are elitist and out of touch".

Yet eight years later Clinton revealed that she actually shared his world view with her unbelievable "deplorables" outburst. She was a worthy successor in title to Obama, as they both shared the same elitist condescension of ordinary people and never thought of them as voters to be won over. Trump certainly did, and his vision proved a necessary corrective to the drift and "declinism" of the Obama years.

The term, "populism", is usually a put-down, implying superficial and opportunistic politics. The reality of the Trump assault was much deeper. He was responding to fundamental grievances affecting the lives of swathes of hard-working middle class Americans, the backbone of a successful society.

The extraordinary success of American exceptionalism was not based on notions of elitism or expanding the welfare state, but of unrelenting aspiration and hard work in a can-do society.

The frustration of the masses, so successfully tapped into by Trump, was based on an instinctive awareness of economic decline. Obama may have inspired many with his soaring rhetoric, for a time anyway, but at heart he remained a community organiser and undergraduate debater, with no commercial or real life business experience and little interest in, or understanding of, economics – long on emotion, short on reason. Clinton saw nothing wrong with this (or perhaps was afraid of an Obama backlash if she took him on), and the public instinctively realised they were being offered more of same.

The contrast with Trump is instructive: a hardened and successful businessman and political outsider competing against another commercial and economic neophyte and professional political careerist. Real life, in contrast to political, experience, is vital for those who aim to be successful leaders. A background in politics can be very useful for getting a foot on the ladder – numbers men are a conspicuous example. But to progress to high levels it is essential to have a broader, more worldly outlook.

Trump may have been a political arriviste but, like Bob Hawke, who also came to electoral politics relatively late, his CV reeked of relevant skills. He got off to a good start with an economics degree from the prestigious Wharton Business School, whose alumni include Warren Buffett and Elon Musk. By age 25 he was running the family real estate business, already re-branded The Trump Organisation.

For the next 45 years he dramatically expanded its operations into major building projects – skyscrapers, hotels, casinos, golf courses, with the Trump brand emblazoned all over. The US construction sector is notoriously, even threateningly, competitive, requiring intestinal fortitude and tough negotiating skills to prosper or even to survive. Setbacks, even bankruptcies, along the way are common, sometimes inevitable.

High-level decision-making experience was an invaluable asset. Coming to politics after a lifetime of crisis management and making big calls in a precarious environment is an ideal preparation. In addition, he had also spent many years in the media and entertainment business, polishing his image and becoming a household name as producer and host for more than ten years of *The Apprentice*.

As a result, his current net worth according to *Forbes Magazine* is around $US 3.5 billion, putting him in the top 600 richest people in the world. The public instinctively know you do not reach these heights by luck, or by being a clown. You have to be one very smart operator.

He had spent his life doing deals and striking bargains – again, shades of Bob Hawke. But, unlike in the Australian system, he was able to bring into government many high achievers from the private sector, albeit individually, for quite short stints. As all Australian ministers have to be drawn from the ranks of parliamentarians, the best we can do is for the two major parties to make a conscious effort to preselect persons of potential, even if not proven expertise, preferably from the private sector, the engine room of the economy, where the vast majority of voters reside.

Trump the person

As for many Australians, indeed many Americans, Donald Trump, the person, is not my cup of tea. With the morals of an alley cat and the language of a gutter snipe, he is a true vulgarian who fails the character test, big time. But, if we went around shunning leaders we did not like or did not agree with, we would fast run out of interlocutors.

Voters are not used to political rudeness – politicians try to court them politely, sometimes with unctuous phrases, while desperately pandering to the media. No one has ever accused Trump of being polite or of pandering to anyone. It would go against the habits of a lifetime.

He revels in risk-taking and brinkmanship, happy to shut down the US government for a time. He is often compared to the mercurial Andrew Jackson, seventh president of the United States (1829-37), a fiery frontiersman and military hero, who also seemed to thrive on criticism and loved a fight. Did Trump care that he was a hate figure to millions and the devil incarnate to his political opponents? No, he thrived on it.

The US system of checks and balances provided him with political creature comforts such as a virtually guaranteed four-year term, something a political isolate like Malcolm Turnbull would have died for. When I read *The Art of the Deal* more than 30 years ago, the braggadocio had not yet surfaced, but it was clear that he was not short on self-confidence.

Yet more than 63 million voted for him in November 2016, some, presumably many women, with little suppressed distaste. Four years later he had added another ten million votes . Clearly he was on to something, even if the commentators could not or would not understand what it was. Some of his detractors now concede that while he may have been a charlatan, the deep socio-economic causes of Trumpism are real. How else to explain why one out of two women and one out of three Latinos voted for the Donald.

For the great majority, he presented a once in a lifetime political opportunity to turn the tables on the rich and famous, the intellectual elites, the condescending academics, the insular media, the captains of industry and the "inside the beltway" types who form the Washington establishment, and all those who had looked down on, or had just ignored, middle America for so long.

The G20 group, of which Australia is a member, has been advocating lower direct taxes for a decade as the most effective way of kick-starting an economy and generating more jobs. It has also argued for largescale, deficit-financed infrastructure. Trump was quick to follow suit. Similarly, reducing the size of government, by cutting back on largely out of control, Obama-created regulation, did wonders for employment creation by aiding corporate productivity.

Clinton would have none of this, ignoring polls which showed, by more than two to one, that Americans believed the country was on the wrong track. She vowed instead to defend Obama's "legacy" of anti-business regulation and growth-stifling energy policies, and to double down on job-killers like Obamacare, the fastest growing entitlement program of all.

She surely won few friends among uncommitted voters by echoing Obama in insisting that Islam had nothing to do with terrorism and denouncing any expressions of unease about Islam as "Islamophobia". She should have known better. Even her husband had said publicly nine months out from the campaign: "It's time to put the awful legacy of the last eight years behind us."

The lessons of history

The Trump "revolt of the masses" did not come out of the blue. The Brexit referendum, less than five months earlier, provided ample warning of the likelihood of the voice of the financially depressed mainstream becoming ascendant. Even the British election of 2015 was a shock to most commentators who thought it was about everything except the issue that always preoccupies voters, the legendary hip pocket nerve.

Constant repetition of bread and butter issues may not sell newspapers or excite their editors but, as one of the Tories' leading campaign strategists put it: "Every day not spent in campaigning on the economy is a day wasted."

In large part the media repeatedly misread the play by listening to the wrong people. Their *modus operandi* is to solicit quotes from the articulate, many with an axe to grind or a position to defend. Seek out opinions from "the usual suspects", spokesmen and women for various peak bodies, captains of industry, the Governor of the Bank of England, and on it goes. The media are also usually quick to pretend that each side has equal merit – the vice of political relativism.

Many opponents of Brexit in the business community were doing very nicely out of the status quo. Why not stick with the devil you know rather than take a big leap into the unknown? They visited Europe frequently and enjoyed it immensely, so what was the problem? They did not spend much time in the north of their own country or read newspapers of which they disapproved.

Similarly, in the United States, the great and the good were recovering nicely from the GFC, did not have to struggle for a living, got on well with the political class. Hillaryland was largely populated by residents of Washington, DC, and the wealthy, liberal cities of New York and California – few struggletowns there. The disconnect between Democrat support in these three havens and the rest of the country was canyonesque.

This is the fundamental lesson from the Trump revolution. While a country is prosperous, most people do not pay much attention to politics and are inclined to re-elect the incumbent, although seeking a third term for the same party can be fraught. It has only happened once since the Second World War, when Vice-

President George H. W. Bush succeeded the very popular Ronald Reagan. But, especially in Australia, it is never an "it's time" moment just because of longevity, although the voters can just get sick of incumbents and be up for change.

If anything, the punters give themselves the major credit for their own success. But when things turn bad or stay sluggish for years on end, and they become trapped in a slough of despond, they need someone to be held to account. One of the key questions pollsters ask is: "Do you think the country is going in the right/ wrong direction"; or, as Ronald Reagan memorably put it during his one debate with Jimmy Carter: "Are you better off now than you were four years ago?"

Given the circumstances, it is not hard to see why the struggling lower middle class would choose change ahead of more of the same, especially if the change proponent is offering some dramatic new proposals, as Trump certainly was. Political strategies cannot be developed in a vacuum, or based on a rigid reading of past experience, they must respond to the here and now, to people's present needs and wants.

Academics and political commentators have a notoriously bad record in politics. They tend to believe they know the reasons for all the past triumphs and failures but, in most instances, they are simply fighting the last war (which they probably got wrong, anyway), despite politics being a very fast-moving game.

Much is made of Trump's anti-trade rhetoric, unequivocally bad for business and therefore bad politics. But if the long-standing political reality is that the American working class believed that it was disproportionately bearing the burden of globalisation and free trade deals, which send their jobs offshore, perhaps it is understandable that an aspiring president felt compelled to do something to address these fears.

After all, less than half of adult Americans have full-time jobs and a sixth of adult American men are involuntarily idle. Millions feel consigned to low productivity, low paid jobs for life. Illegal immigration and the consequent job losses are very emotional issues for these people.

Free trade may be a tried and proven formula in Western economies, but it is more appreciated by those with a macro view than those on the ground who may be its unwitting victims. One of America's foremost foreign affairs commentators, Walter Russell Mead, whilst warning that protectionism remains a "dangerous drug" which could disrupt America's alliances, even as it drags down domestic economic growth, nonetheless points out that the rules of the game have changed because "countries like China and Russia have weaponised investment and trade to advance their revisionist agendas".

It follows that the US and its allies cannot just ignore the extent to which this aberrant behaviour has disrupted Western economic assumptions. Mead concludes that whilst populists do not offer answers to such complex problems, Trump's concerns could not safely be ignored in a democratic society.

Trump's style

Around 25 million households and 50 million people, mostly white, receive food stamps. Trump's 2016 victory showed that Americans did not want to be a nation of layabouts; they wanted America to be great again, As Soon As Possible. Before he was halfway through his first term, unemployment was already down to a 17-year low of 3.9%.

A characteristic example of the ivory tower "forget the politics, just do the right thing" crowd is *The Economist*, once a serious economic journal, now little more than an international current affairs magazine, in the style of the now defunct *Newsweek*. It presumably supports democracy, but not the accompanying pragmatic decisions that make politics "the art of the possible". It airily dismisses these middle class concerns as "the unfocused resentment of globalisation and its hoity-toity champions, harboured by many working-class Americans."

It goes on: "The result is an emotional and self-regarding critique of America's imperfect but precious trade architecture that appears largely waterproofed against economic reality". This lazy diatribe ill becomes a journal which used to be admired for its economic insights, but now seems to prefer to slag off from the sidelines at intellectually inferior know-nothings such as Trump.

Trump was once a Democrat. Now he is a Republican – sort of. All the evidence is that he is not an ideologue, but a pragmatist who, like any self-respecting businessman, wanted to get things done, make things work and make some real money. If he could have changed sentiment amongst trading partners and also bring jobs back home via his tax plan, it is highly likely that he would, in due course, have reverted to more conventional trade policy. His America First agenda may not have been "nice", but it was rational and coherent. After all, any democratic country, not to mention some which are not, which did not put its own interests first, would be letting its citizens down.

He expressed his ambition in his inaugural address in strong, emotional and powerful terms which, in principle, we should all be able to accept:

> From this day forward, a new vision will govern our land. From this moment on, it's going to be America first. We must protect our borders from the ravages of other countries making our products, stealing our companies and destroying our jobs.

The loudest objections came from internationalists who wanted the United States to continue to expend vast sums on keeping the world safe, so they could decry it for acting like a global policeman. Meanwhile NATO continued to get a free ride on US coat-tails.

What Trump was proposing was a time-honoured, conservative, small government agenda: protecting the vulnerable, putting the country first, defending the people, creating jobs, looking after families – the antithesis of the Clinton devotion to identity politics and grievance culture.

It was an approach aimed directly at the heartland, with comparable appeal in Australia. As Australia's foremost political commentator, Paul Kelly, pointed out, as soon as Trump was elected, his victory signalled a revolt against the identity politics of the Obama era, its pervasive agenda of political correctness and its determination to end discrimination against all manner of minority groups.

Trump offered a fundamentally different moral vision. He strongly opposed the growing trend towards cultural liberalism and moral relativism, advocating a return to traditional values (most of which he preached rather than practised) and a practical concern for all, and not only special treatment for some. The liberal orthodoxy of celebrating cultural differences had become a wedge driving society apart.

This warning is highly relevant to Australia, where victimology and the right not to be offended have become running sores, a consequence, in large part of the narrow preoccupations of the Australian Human Rights Commission, especially under the former presidency of Professor Gillian Triggs. To date, this divisive creed has been largely confined to the Greens. But the ALP, fearful of becoming the road kill of its former coalition allies in inner suburban enclaves, is still tempted to follow them down this dangerous path, which risks losing the mainstream in the process.

Master of the new politics

Having built his own mega empire and being an expert in the information and entertainment industries, Trump knew the powerful leverage of social media, which could reach millions, particularly the younger demographic, in real time. The hordes who check their phones hourly would be constantly bombarded with messages that old time TV could never deliver.

Many times a day Trump could compose a ten second, from-the-heart, text message, with no journalistic "translation", and millions could see and share it. Social media became his primary communications vehicle, using a direct cut through and often entertaining style, linking the medium to the message as the Canadian communications guru, Marshall McLuhan, had long ago enjoined. Trump became a one-man megaphone, unfiltered by advisers, who are often as much interested in protecting themselves as their master.

He knew what mattered when it came to capturing the voter's attention. Conventional TV debates are beloved of old style journalists who react to every twitch and parse every phrase for the benefit of a relatively small number of ageing readers.

But those debates are almost always transient events – here today, sunk without trace tomorrow – unlike Twitter, which was forever in the faces of millions. Clinton may have known her brief and rarely put a conventional foot wrong until the "deplorables" fiasco, but she simply could not compete with the raw power of Trump's genuine, often brutal, language.

Her words, no doubt carefully crafted by speech writers, were mere sanitised verbiage, of little interest to the masses, whom Trump knew needed to be entertained, even outraged, not just informed, let alone hectored. With Trump you got the genuine article, misspellings and all, no political correctness thrown in.

Clinton was concerned not to say anything wrong. Trump thrived on it. The media take out was that he was disorganised, messy and undisciplined, when the reality was that he was cunning, strategic and deliberate. He did not care how many objected; the more the merrier. He was quick to abuse his critics and the punters loved it, just as they empathised with a politician who was game to take on the media monolith.

Many politicians may have dreamed of doing so, but their advisers would have told them it would be a catastrophic mistake, because journalists would object and take revenge. But Trump was not looking for the plaudits of journalists.

He wanted to connect with real people, and he knew that if they agreed with him (and this was carefully monitored) they would re-tweet to others, thereby delivering ever more unpaid publicity. Although Trump had several million more followers than his opponent – a big starting advantage – it would ultimately have counted for little if he had not used it effectively with cut-through lines, no BS, just words and phrases that everyone could understand.

He deliberately picked fights because he knew the media could not resist controversy and thrived on negativity and criticism. So, unwittingly, or unavoidably, they did his job for him. They screamed, "look, yet another gaffe"; he responded, "thanks, yet more free publicity". The mainstream media saw "building a wall" and "repealing Obamacare" as breathtakingly outrageous and offensive mistakes, whereas his base heard the message and were enthused by it. They admired his fearlessness – a wild west hero taking on the cavalry.

At no stage did the media read the play, let alone get the "joke." Instead, they tried their best to rein him in. They railed against his constant twitterisms, urging him to give it a break. He knew better; he ignored them. He also knew they found his outrages journalistically irresistible, so his messages ended up in the mainstream media, without even trying. He chose the topics under discussion and the media had to follow along. He did not have to explain or elaborate; the less said, the more they could argue over the meaning, thus fuelling his fire.

His tweets, spontaneous, unfiltered, from the heart, provided unique insights into his feelings, creating empathy in the process, and allowing his followers to believe they knew the real him. Authenticity is critical. As Hollywood comedian and actor George

Burns was fond of saying: "Sincerity – if you can fake that, you've got it made." But no one thought this was a manufactured Donald speaking; it reeked of the real thing.

Another huge benefit of his approach was that he got enormous traction for a fraction of the amount his rivals spent. Whilst Clinton reportedly outspent him three to one on television, some have assessed the effective unpaid cost of his social media spend at $2-3 billion. The key to understanding, if not liking, Trump's genius was that he transformed the contest by being more entertaining and generating more passion. He was also aided by rapid technological change, which enabled his followers to forward their likes to friends, thus creating a whole new audience, again free of charge.

An important lesson for politicians elsewhere, including Australia, is be brave, or at least confident, believe in yourself and not the polls, make sure you deliver to your target audience, then give them some tasty morsels to chew on – things which matter to them such as sound economics or cheaper electricity prices. Most importantly, deliver it in language they can relate to.

It does not have to be a litany of big hairy policies. The trick is to address people's needs, not offer what you think might be good for them. And do not be afraid to stand firm, even in the face of heavy criticism. In 2019, Scott Morrison met all these requirements. In many ways he was fortunate to have a Clinton-like opponent – an out-of-touch and over-confident Shorten – disliked, even distrusted, up against Morrison, a down-to-earth and likeable friend of the battlers.

Getting the message out to those who mattered

In order to appreciate the scale of the Trump achievement fully it is necessary to understand the extent to which he departed from the conventional approach adopted by his opponents on all sides. The standard *modus operandi* for winning office has been to present policies which offer moderate change but do not unsettle too many people. If the level of outrage rises too high the instinctive reaction is to try to close the issue down before someone suggests it was all a mistake, leading the rest of the media to conclude, sheep-like, that the candidate has faltered.

In other words, conventional campaign strategies rely on gaining media approval, not necessarily appealing directly to voters. The premise is that the media will determine the outcome by generating momentum and the voters will obediently take their cue from them. This was the insider's game which Trump turned monumentally on its head. In doing so he exposed the media's ultimate lack of political influence and power of persuasion.

Look at his signature policies:

- a total and complete shutdown of Muslims entering the United States;
- build a border wall with Mexico and make Mexico pay for it;
- stop illegal immigration and deport an estimated 11 million unauthorised Mexican immigrants;
- dismantle Obamacare and replace it with "something terrific";
- cut the corporate tax rate from 35% to 15% and introduce "massive" tax cuts for working and middle-income Americans;
- withdraw from the Paris Accord on climate change and revive the Keystone XL pipeline project;
- appoint conservative pro-life judges to the Supreme Court;
- withdraw from the Trans-Pacific Partnership and re-negotiate the North American Free Trade Agreement.

At their essence his core offerings were all about economics and security: make America economically strong again, make America secure again. His trade policies were all about jobs, as were his pitches to wind back regulations and provide more and cheaper energy.

None of these dramatic initiatives would have occurred to any Democrat contenders for whom core business has usually been, at least notionally, improving the lives of the lowest income Americans. Their valid expectation is that the largely left-leaning media will applaud such measures as part of a fairness agenda and a tangible step towards reducing inequality and inequities. Until Trump arrived to fracture the mould, no one seemed to want to cater for the middle ground, a much bigger voting cohort than the lower income demographic, many of whom do not even vote.

Apart from the immediate voter attractiveness, these were bigger issues in play, in fact, a wide philosophical chasm was opening up. Trump's measures were aimed squarely at rebuilding the American economy and creating new jobs, whereas the Democrat focus was, once again, on wealth redistribution. After eight years of an anti-big business President, much more interested in sharing than creating wealth, this was like a breath of fresh air to many millions who had long yearned for mainstream policies even if, at times, crudely presented.

Each of these was breathtaking in scope. It is one thing to promise reform – the typical middle of the road politician's response would be: "I am determined to do something about Muslim immigration, restrict the flow of Mexicans into the US and fix up the health system."

But NO: the Trump way was to inflate these issues by the use of supersized rhetoric, designed to make everyone sit up and take notice. Moreover, in the face of an outpouring of fury and disbelief from the liberal press, he simply doubled down, not condescending to provide any level of detail.

This undoubtedly annoyed the media, not used to someone ripping up the long-standing rules of the game and treating them with disdain. But it did not faze Trump, and it electrified his campaign. Voters want to know why they should vote for a candidate. Here was an unconventional politician, behaving as no politician had behaved in living memory, offering a clear and unvarnished set of promises; the ultimate dog whistle in the sense that he wanted them to get the message, not parse the statement. This assessment fits the public choice theory of Nobel Prize winning economist, James Buchanan, that people's self-interest is the principal determinant of voting behaviour.

The furious response from the great and the good, liberal economists and fellow travellers, and Trump's provocative, don't-give-an-inch response, was music to the ears of the many who were not used to political debates being conducted in terms they could relate to.

They liked the punch up, silently identifying with a serious contender, saying what many of them thought about the media, and they liked his policy approach even more. This was not apparent to most journalists, who simply took every word at face value and spent an inordinate amount of time cataloguing every inaccurate statement, of which there were many.

The voters had become heartily sick of the pusillanimous, "compassionate" approach of Obama and, to a lesser extent, Clinton. They saw much time, money and sympathy being spent on uninvited guests, and little spent on themselves.

The best apophthegm of the campaign came from a relatively unknown columnist, Salena Zito, with her now immortal line that the press had taken Trump literally but not seriously, while his backers had taken his statements seriously but not literally.

"The Wall" was a real and solid structure for the media, immediately provoking a thousand questions, which conveniently filled up a lot of space: Who will build it? What will it cost? Who will pay for it, etc, etc?

But, for voters, "The Wall" was a metaphor, a colourful way of explaining that he was willing to do something dramatic about the biggest issue of all and do his best to turn back the flow of illegal immigrants who were causing social disharmony and becoming disconcerting to so many.

The validity of Zito's pithy and insightful assessment has not been seriously contested and has been endlessly quoted ever since. She is a national reporter who resides in rural Pennsylvania. Like Warren Buffett, she lives far from the madding crowd, where she can retain professional detachment.

I had the same feeling as I travelled through the key mid-west states of Pennsylvania, Ohio, Indiana and Michigan en route to Cleveland, with very few Clinton placards and not too much overt political pageantry. My quick tour provided a fascinating glimpse of mainly white middle class and, presumably, mainstream, Americans. No "support gender equality and critical race theory" posters there!

Over the years I have attended political party conferences in a number of countries and too many to count in the Australian states. But I have never been to one where all the "big beasts", as the British call top-tier politicians, were alienated in varying degrees of antipathy from their de facto party leader. The various commentators, journalists, political pundits and groupies hanging around the Convention were united in their view that Trump was unelectable.

In a fortuitous piece of good timing, which coincided with Zito's assessment, a Gallup Poll reported the lowest approval rating ever for the media, with less than one-third saying they had a great deal or even a fair amount of trust in the very journalistic pack that had assailed Trump's legitimacy at every turn. Ironically, this underlined the astuteness and courage of Trump's devastating media assault; he was pushing at an open door as far as middle America was concerned. Since forever, the media had assumed they could bully, harass or humiliate candidates into toeing their line. Now Trump was hitting back with devastating force and bursting their bubble in a very public way.

Campaign and victory

What is truly surprising now, nearly more than years after Trump's 2016 electoral triumph, is how many people continued to deny his legitimacy and treated his victory as an unfortunate mishap, albeit that whilst he lost in 2020, he got 11 million votes more than the previous time. There was an almost complete failure to comprehend that there has been a major change in American politics. No longer would whitebread candidates be able to safely pander to the pet issues of a media much more interested in colour, movement and novelty than what concerns ordinary voters.

Donald Trump has never acted like a politician or cared much about elite or even "educated" opinion. It has always been taken for granted that politicians must cosy up to the media; alienate them at your peril. Staffers are always on hand to remind their superiors in every interview to be very careful not to put a foot or a word wrong. Trump, to their distress, simply tore up this time-honoured script.

For him, the Marquess of Queensberry rules were out and Rafferty's rules prevailed. Trump did not seem to care what the media thought. Most of his supporters thoroughly enjoyed the sacrilege. In reality, he almost certainly knew exactly what he was doing. He has almost certainly changed the political landscape forever, even as his multitude of critics continue to assume that he was an aberration, with normal transmission to be resumed as soon as the buffoon had been dispatched.

The real lesson from the Trump tsunami is that he defied doubters and doomsayers by appealing over their heads, and the punters responded in spades. No doubt he benefitted from Clinton's underlying fragility, but nonetheless he only won because he offered a very real alternative to the status quo.

The contest was always going to be hers to lose, given the awesome war chest at her disposal and her past-the-post media status, but there should have been lingering doubts, from the same front runner position she lost the Democrat nomination in 2008 to another rank outsider, Barack Obama. The Clintons had many admirers, but Hillary clearly lacked Bill's charisma and was not trusted by significant numbers. Now here she was, the safety first, risk averse candidate, who preferred to stay largely beneath the radar, brimming with overconfidence, trotting out her centre-left bromides, and not bothering to campaign in what she thought were locked up states.

Trump strategists no doubt always thought they were in with a show. We will never know how confident they really were, but there are few certainties in politics and a perennial high achiever like Trump was never going to die wondering.

Team Trump seemed content to keep quiet and preserve their candidate's status as the rank outsider, while all the time pedalling furiously beneath the surface. The traditional media experts scoffed at his campaign as a family affair of enthusiastic amateurs, implying that no one else was willing to be co-opted to the losing side.

No one bothered to check Jared Kushner's imposing commercial record, or his capacity to master a brief, as the digital mastermind behind the campaign. Trump's history of outsize business success was waved aside in preference to the view that a parvenu like him would be simply unable to compete with the awesome Clinton machine.

If the pundits had looked, they would have seen how, late in 2015 in Canada, the Liberal Party under Justin Trudeau, son of Pierre Elliott Trudeau, not flush with funds, had surfed to victory in Canada on social media, despite not being flush with funds. He had ousted a successful leader, the Conservative Stephen Harper, prime minister since 2006, just as Kevin Rudd had ousted Howard in Australia in 2007.

The achievements of these long-serving and largely successful leaders no longer cut the mustard. The public had simply tired of political longevity and wanted a change. It could have been different if the 2007 Australian election had been fought in the depths of the GFC, when voters might well have preferred a safe pair of hands; we will never know.

By contrast with Harper and Howard, Obama had put in eight lacklustre years on the policy front, as far as the middle class were concerned, and here was Hillary Clinton offering more of the same. Why was it assumed that a multi-billionaire, with a ravenous appetite for power, offering dramatic change and with the latest technology at his disposal, would not be able to take a digital strategy to new heights?

The battle for the Presidency was almost universally regarded as a David and Goliath contest: yes, as it turned out, it was, but in reverse. Trump virtually ignored the traditional press, understandable given that only two of the top 100 circulation print newspapers endorsed him. But he had the last laugh, as the media barons were utterly humiliated by a result virtually none had picked.

The media tend to be very influenced by public opinion polls, which they use as a security blanket to express confident ex post facto opinions and, in some cases, to validate their political prejudices. In my time there were journalists (some of whom are still around) who simply could not conceal their distaste for right-of-centre politicians.

The trouble is that sophisticated polling, even confined in Australia's case to some 20 key marginal electorates, is too expensive for the media to undertake on a systematic basis – faster and cheaper to get away with a nationwide poll, although at best a weak average and not a reliable guide, as the 2019 Australian Federal election showed.

Most rank and file journalists are little more than armchair commentators. If they did talk and mix with real people, the people in the suburbs, in the shopping centres and the factories, the regional towns, and rural Australia, instead of only to colleagues and the like-minded, they would have a chance of being much better directly informed, and able to sniff the mood, catch the real zeitgeist.

The real take-away from the Trump tsunami is that he defied doubters and doomsayers by appealing over their heads. The punters responded in spades, even in 2020.

Remember, the media is not there to be helpful; they exist to sell, not even to report. Hence their writers now prefer to be labelled journalists, not reporters.

The lesson for any political party in a democracy wanting to win office is clear: cultivate the mainstream, even if you secretly do not share all their values, because that is where the majority of the votes always are.

6

The Mainstream Media

An epic fail

Much election-time journalism is of the desktop variety, recycling already written words and throwing in a few "strategic insights". There is occasionally a foray onto the campaign trail in the company of a candidate's team and talking to a few vox pop volunteers. As a result, during American presidential campaigns, there is little real reporting from the front lines. In endless discussion of battleground states and national polls, there are few attempts to understand the attitudes and thinking, let alone likely voting patterns, of middle America.

It was not until after the 2016 election that anyone noticed that Hillary Clinton had not paid a single visit to Wisconsin, presumably because it was thought to be in the bag. Abundant financial and human resources notwithstanding, the Clinton camp (with the exception of Bill, whose views were frequently overruled by camp "experts") seemed to be blissfully unaware that almost the entire Midwest was up for grabs. The awareness of the media was little better.

The catastrophic media failure to anticipate the election outcome in 2016, or to get much more than the winner right in 2020, simply demonstrated a fundamental disconnect between the comfortable media elite and the real world. This is partly owing to cost and partly to laziness. If the media had really wanted to understand and report on the likely course and outcome of the campaigns, they would have spent serious money on some in-depth, state-by-state polling and research analysis. But it is much easier, and cheaper, to rely on small samples or simplistic nationwide polls and extrapolate from these inherently unreliable measures.

The media know that the electoral outcome in a presidential election in the United States is determined by the results in less than ten "battleground" states, but they rarely bother to canvas this bloc. Instead, they prefer to play games like "Texas is usually a safe Republican state, but this time it could turn blue". It did not.

60 million people, some 18% of the national population, reside in two states, California and New York. Both are safe Democrat strongholds. As a result, it makes little sense for the Republicans to waste resources there, so their true level of support is understated, and that of their opponents accordingly overstated. This inevitably distorts the so-called popular vote, which has nothing to do with the electoral college outcome. Yet the media are happy to report these meaningless aggregate statistics, as though the winner of the popular vote is morally the deserving winner, and the electoral college system a flawed measure, even when they know that the Founding Fathers knew exactly what they were doing.

Unfortunately, the polls act as a safety blanket for many commentators. As a consequence, they often make skewed predictions in line with trends in the polls rather than on the merits, creating a mood which may well be wildly inaccurate.

In the 2019 Australian Federal election, because there was no widespread or sustained public outrage against Labor's proposals to abolish franking credits and double the capital gains tax, the commentators simply assumed that the polls were vindicating Labor's plans, when clearly the voters, having consulted their tax advisers, were quietly seething.

The same pattern of fundamentally misreading the play was repeated in the 2020 presidential campaign, albeit with some understandable caution, the media having been badly burned last time. But they did not seem to have learned much. Right in predicting a Biden victory, they nevertheless erroneously assumed that Trump would be obliterated. Once again they completely failed to understand the reason for his magnetic appeal, when most of the elites could not stand the man.

The furious response from the great and the good, liberal economists and fellow travellers, to Trump's provocative, do not-give-an-inch mouthings, was, once again, music to the ears of many who were not used to political debates being conducted in terms they could relate to.

They liked the punch up, silently identifying with a serious contender saying what many of them thought about the media. And they liked his policy approach even more. This was not apparent to most journalists, who simply took every word at face value and spent an inordinate amount of time cataloguing every inaccurate statement, of which there were many. He could change the national conversation with one deliberately outrageous tweet and the media were powerless to resist the siren call of outrage; this simply played into his hands.

Trump's assault on US media outlets, many of whom he accused of being unpatriotic and often dishonest, was very disruptive and sent the major players into overdrive. That was the object of the exercise. In many respects it was also long overdue.

CNN, created by "Hanoi Jane" Fonda's erstwhile husband and political soulmate, Ted Turner, and his ilk, had had the field largely to themselves for decades until Rupert Murdoch identified a yawning gap in the television political landscape and created Fox News, for whom Trump was particularly fertile ground. His take-no-prisoners approach struck a deep chord with millions whose views had been mocked by the left-wing media for many years.

Vigorous presidential disagreements with the press are nothing new, dating back to the time of George Washington who took furious exception to the behaviour of newspaper editor Philip Freneau. Not long afterwards, while under siege from the press, the third president, Thomas Jefferson, felt compelled to say: "Nothing can now be believed which is seen in a newspaper. Truth itself becomes suspicious by being put into that polluted vehicle."

Several years after leaving office, President Harry Truman opined that, "when the press is friendly to an administration the opposition had been lied about and treated to the excrescences of paid prostitutes of the mind".

In many ways politicians and the press are natural adversaries, the former constantly seeking good news stories, the latter the opposite. But, while the days of the "yellow" or "gutter" press are largely behind us, the media landscape should not be a lawless jungle where anything goes. A civilised society is entitled to expect that the media will themselves promote rational discourse, with a due concern for fairness and objectivity. Without it we are all the losers.

The question still remains, how did everyone get it so wrong, even the hitherto infallible statistician, Nate Silver, who had successfully called the outcomes in 49 of the 50 states in the 2008 US Presidential election and went one better four years later? His 2016 election forecast had Hillary Clinton with a 71.4% chance of winning, with Donald Trump languishing on 28.6%, and facing the biggest landslide in the history of presidential contests. Silver, as it happens, was closer than most.

The *Huffington Post*, which in 2016 only reported on Trump in its entertainment section, had Clinton past the post at 98.2%; and the *New York Times* had her at an unbackable 85%. Every other major forecaster had similar figures. The whole thing was a devastating indictment of the press but, as one of the benefits of being a club member is never having to say you are sorry, the great bulk of the post-mortem analysis stayed well clear of hanging the main culprits.

Politics and the media are almost always on a collision course. Many in the media generally earn a living by discovering new outrages and scandals and, today, endlessly pursuing trendy issues of gender, political correctness, equality and diversity, which are of little interest to mainstream voters. This is not necessarily the media's fault, as an unrelieved diet of bread and butter economic issues is unlikely to boost newspaper sales or excite reader fury. The "success" of social media lies in the fact that everyone can be an expert on social issues and venting often provides a useful way of letting off steam. But very few are enlightened and it is highly unlikely to change the world view of most voters.

Focus groups will understandably tell pollsters and their fellow participants that they do not like negative advertising. The media are happy to pretend that this professed voter preference for the positive should dictate political party campaign strategy, when they know full well that negative advertising works, especially when it confirms people's instincts and prejudices.

Positive messages are too often dismissed as propaganda unless they come from independent third parties with no obvious axe to grind. The Australian political system is very clean and honourable by international standards. Yet because the media thrives on skulduggery and scandal, such as the misdeeds of former NSW Labor ministers Eddie Obeid, Joe Tripodi and Ian MacDonald, these infrequent episodes quickly become egregious examples of a flawed political class. A single instance is often generalised as the "tip of the iceberg" example of a systemic, deep-rooted cultural problem.

It is so much easier for a political practitioner to impugn the integrity or question the motives of a political opponent than engage in a serious debate, which the media are unlikely to report in depth. It is simpler to run with political invective or well-crafted put-downs in the expectation that this is the best way to catch the attention of voters. It also makes for much more florid and saleable headlines. Time and again the media deliberately avoid explaining what a political argument is really about. In a wages dispute, often all the readership is told is the extent of any actual or potential disruption, rarely the core of the dispute, such as the impact on costs of a big wage increase.

The "vice" of the one-liner is not new: Julius Caesar and William Shakespeare were but two notable exponents of the art. Then, as now, it can be devastatingly effective as it helps to crystallise a political proposition. But recent inventions such as Twitter, an ingenious dumbing down device, compound the mendacity of political exchange by facilitating little more than a crude exchange of prejudices.

The idea that political parties have to reach out and cater for swinging voters is another seductive but flawed construct. It assumes that this group is a discrete cohort, whereas their interests and concerns are almost certainly mainstream. So the concentration should be on finding a broadly popular policy which works more for the many than the few. But the media often like to pretend otherwise.

Another favourite, but simplistic, media game is to pretend that there is an obvious middle ground between two warring political proposals and it is only jockeying for political advantage that prevents reason and common sense from prevailing. Often big philosophical and strategic differences are at stake, particularly on the international stage.

Should Australia refrain from addressing concerns about increasing militarisation in the South China Sea simply to avoid offending the claimed sensitivities of one of the major players? Certainly megaphone diplomacy should generally be eschewed in favour of serious concerns being raised effectively through diplomatic channels, but the alternative cannot be a vow of silence.

The lamentations: commentators in denial

After Trump's 2016 victory one prominent New York professor of journalism went further than most, lamenting, "the mere fact of Trump's candidacy is evidence of the failure of journalism." This perhaps is not surprising, coming from a denizen of one of the few rock solid Democrat strongholds, but it is still breathtaking in its disdain, even contempt, for the outcome of a free and fair election, the essence of modern democracy. Such pundits simply cannot accept that anyone in their right mind could hold what they consider to be neanderthal views. The reality was that it was evidence of the failure of the left-wing media and commentators to sell a dodgy bill of goods to a savvy voting public.

Many commentators remain in denial more than four years after Trump's 2016 triumph. They blame everything associated with Trump for his defeat in 2020, ignoring the enduring appeal of Trumpism which ensured that there was no landslide. Middle America was still quite conservative, but a sufficient number were sick of the outrageous behaviour of Trumpism's principal proponent and happy to vote for anyone but.

The antidote for sufferers of TDS (Trump Derangement Syndrome) is to get out more often. Then they might understand that swathes of the population, instead of being appalled, as right-thinking elites and comfortable professionals were, actually identified with what they were watching, reading and hearing.

The operating assumption of elites was that Trump was a loose-tongued, dim-witted amateur, who just spat out whatever vile inanities came into his silly head. Whilst a deal of his vitriol was personally hurtful and racially offensive, there can be little doubt that his language and his presentation were a key part of a calculated approach.

Just as importantly, it almost certainly reflected his own personal views and prejudices which he knew, from his life experience, were shared by many millions, but who were not willing or able to say so. He deliberately made what many considered xeno-phobic and nationalistic attacks the centrepiece of his campaign, as he clearly understood that hostility towards immigration and globalisation ran deep among a critical mass of voters.

Media groupthink

The major newspapers, in both their print and digital forms, still have a considerable if declining influence on their readers' political views. It is a safe bet, however, that their principal readers are elites like themselves. Trump voters living in non-urban areas are unlikely to be avid readers. Indeed, their voting behaviour in recent years suggests that if they do read such information sources they do not take much notice of them and are happy to reject their overwhelmingly anti-Trump world-view.

It should always be remembered that private sector media organisations are commercial entities who must make a profit or go out of business. They therefore pitch their message to cater for an identifiable reader/viewer predilection. That is how they earn a living.

Surprisingly, this is not always the case nowadays. Following the recent New Zealand election, when more than half the voting population did not support Prime Minister Jacinda Ardern, all four daily newspapers effusively supported the winner. As Nick Cater later pointed out in an insightful article in *The Australian*: "We can only conclude that commercial logic no longer applies. Media companies are no longer driven by the pursuit of unserved segments of the market" – in this case the other 50% who did not vote for the winner.

In Western countries, where free markets and freedom of speech is still an article of faith for the majority, the media are a fiercely contested space, unless you are a protected and well-funded public broadcaster. And, like nature, media abhor a vacuum. The *Wall Street Journal* recently celebrated the arrival of a formidable competitor to Twitter and its partisan agenda. In defiance of cancel culture activists, and proud to commit to the letter and spirit of the First Amendment, Parler promised an open platform: "We prefer to leave decisions about what is seen and who is heard to each individual."

As with politics, the media world can be divided into two basic camps. On the one side there are those whose primary concerns are economic and financial and have a practical/realistic outlook, driven by their experience and personal circumstances, what economists call a positive view. Their favourite media outlet in the United States is the business-focused *Wall Street Journal*, America's largest weekday newspaper with print circulation almost double that of its nearest competitor.

On the other hand, there are those more concerned about social issues, more idealistic than pragmatic, greatly concerned about climate change, inequality, discrimination, racial injustice and a shopping list of social justice issues, with a normative world-view of how the world ought to be and not particularly concerned with any short term political palliatives to address current needs, but rather a semi-anonymous "big picture" approach.

These diverse views are adequately catered for in every country with a free press. In Australia it is essentially a split between News Limited and the old Fairfax stable. In the UK the dichotomy is the same, epitomised by *The Telegraph* and the *Daily Mail* v *The Guardian* and the *Financial Times*. In the US the "softer" views are more than catered for by the bulk of the media including the *New York Times* (NYT), the *Washington Post*, *USA TODAY*, the *Los Angeles Times* and all the television networks except Fox.

It is fair to say that during the last four years the *Wall Street Journal* has largely given Trump a tick on performance, especially on jobs, tax reform and foreign policy. At the same time, the *Journal* has also acknowledged his oafish and, at times, outrageous personal behaviour.

Most of the media, however, have been much more troubled about behaviour than results. In the lead-up to the 2020 presidential election, they certainly did not feel the need to offer a practical assessment of the impact of Trump's multitude of policy initiatives in almost every field. Maybe they did not have any coherent criticisms, but in many ways were simply pandering to their market demographic. It is much easier, and often more enjoyable, to read a breezy character assassination than an in-depth policy analysis of a complex issue, particularly if the damnation is confirming an existing disposition.

Take the *New York Times*, supposedly an authoritative newspaper of record, which has been around since forever (actually founded in 1851). Ahead of the 2020 presidential election it delivered what was little more than a philippic against the incumbent president.

Making no pretence at balance or objectivity, the *Post* editorial board penned a vicious tirade headed *Donald Trump: The worst President in Modern History?* Why they bothered to insert a question mark is not clear, but its opening sentence certainly was: "Donald Trump's re-election campaign poses the greatest threat to American democracy since World War II." It continued:

> Mr Trump's ruinous tenure has gravely damaged the United States at home and around the world … The enormity and variety of Mr Trump's misdeeds can feel overwhelming. … In 2016 his bitter account of the nation's ailments struck a chord with many voters. He campaigned as a champion of the ordinary workers but he has governed on behalf of the wealthy.

No supporting evidence, just wild and erroneous assertions aimed at the heart, not the head, supremely disinterested in Trump's largely positive impact on the American economy, let alone on ordinary Americans who had been neglected for so long.

The characterisation of "his bitter account of the nation's ailments" gives the game away, redolent of the sniffy and dismissive tone which is nowadays the stock in trade of *The Economist*. The

New York Times editorial writers must have been very surprised that 74 million voted for Trump in 2020 but, then again, maybe they just did not care. No doubt they expressed the same supreme distaste four years previously. They were simply catering for their chosen demographic, who probably lapped up what was at best a litany of half-truths – no mention of anything positive such as tax reforms resulting in the lowest unemployment rate for many years, trillions of dollars brought back on shore to stimulate the domestic manufacturing sector, a potentially transformational Middle East and traditional values back in vogue.

It is worth reflecting for a moment on the award of a Nobel Peace Prize to Barack Obama in 2009 shortly after his election as President. It was not awarded for any policy accomplishment. It was based on his strong emotional support for fashionable issues such as nuclear proliferation and climate change. Can it ever be imagined the Nobelity (sic), let alone the *New York Times*, even considering Donald Trump for having initiated an unimaginable change in Middle East alliances with the prospect of dramatically reducing tensions in the region? Should not actions speak louder than words, especially in politics?

The *Washington Post*, little better, barely deviated from its 2016 editorial board pre-election advice: *Donald Trump is a unique threat to American democracy*. Writing after the Republican National Convention had formally endorsed him in 2016, the *Washington Post* wrote:

> Donald J. Trump, until now a Republican problem, this week became a challenge the nation must confront and overcome. The real estate tycoon is uniquely unqualified to serve as president ... To the extent he has views, they are wrong in their diagnosis of America's problems and dangerous in their proposed solutions ... A Trump presidency would be dangerous for the nation and the world.

They clearly had no idea what ordinary Americans thought about their long-standing predicament and, again, probably did not care. Like the *New York Times*, they were safely inside their comfort zone, catering for a largely wealthy urban demographic. One thing is certain: no matter how one-sided and misguided such editorials might be, they never feel any obligation to apologise or adapt to the real world. Following the recent election there was again no mention of the huge voter cohort who defied all the *bien pensants* and went for Trump.

The *Washington Post* was in no mood to acknowledge anything positive from the Trump era: "Just cleaning up the wreckage Trump leaves behind could take years" – clearly a deep-seated preference for rhetoric over reality. The *Post* had earlier distinguished itself by "urging lawmakers to vote No on Judge Brett Kavanaugh's confirmation to the Supreme Court". To complete the trifecta of left media, we should have a quick look at a newspaper with a wider circulation. Two weeks before the 2020 election, *USA TODAY* was just as adamant in its anti-Trump views:

> Four years ago the Editorial Board, a (self-styled) ideologically and demographically diverse group of journalists, took sides in the presidential race for the first time since *USA TODAY* was founded in 1982 and urged readers not to vote for Trump. … This year the Editorial Board unanimously supports the election of Joe Biden. … Beset by disease, economic suffering and natural disasters fuelled by a changing climate, the nation is dangerously off course.

That none of the above, even if partly true, was the obvious fault of Donald Trump, did not matter. They were simply content to parrot the factoids that helped to make up a good story.

To be clear, it is perfectly acceptable for media outlets to have an editorial view or even a slant. Indeed, many of their readers and viewers expect some guidance. But what should not be acceptable for major media outlets, all of whom proudly proclaim their excellence and objectivity, is to ignore any semblance of balance and, instead, offer a one-sided diatribe of constant denigration. It is impossible for the media to claim to uphold the highest standards of journalism when they refuse to acknowledge a single positive Trump achievement. In doing so, they are not serving a higher purpose. They are playing the base role of the low grade political activist, a role best left to undergraduate politics and quite unappealing to the silent majority of American voters.

7

The Media's Dirty Secret

Polls skew journalism – badly

The results of the 2020 US presidential election have cast serious doubts over the accuracy and efficacy of public opinion polling.

This follows on from the fiasco in 2016 when virtually no one predicted a Trump victory. The pollsters had promised to get to the bottom of the problem and assured us that all would be well this time. Unfortunately it was not, bringing the whole concept and utility of the process into question.

Whilst the actual prediction of a Biden win was correct, the margin was much less than expected and very disappointing for the Democrats who expected to gain outright control of the Senate and certainly did not expect to lose seats in the House of Representatives and several state legislatures.

Moreover, the predictions in some battleground states were wildly wrong, but all in the same direction, favouring the Democratic candidates to such an extent that they overestimated the Democrat advantage by an average of 4%. In states where polls had favoured Biden, the vote margin went to Trump by around 2.6 additional percentage points. And in Republican states Trump did even better than the polls had indicated – by a whopping 6.4 points.

According to the Pew Research Centre, an independent not-for-profit organisation, the fact that the polling errors were not random, and almost uniformly leaned one way, suggests a systematic set of reasons which Pew puts into four categories:

1. Democratic voters were more easily reachable and more willing than Republican voters to respond to surveys.

2. Not all poll respondents who supported Trump may have been inclined to say so – the "shy Trump voter" syndrome.

3. The polling methodology was defective in that there was an underestimation of the enthusiasm for Trump which led to many such voters being regarded as not likely to vote.

4. The coronavirus pandemic dramatically altered how people intended to vote with Democrats disproportionately concerned about the virus.

Polls are an important part of the democratic political process and all political parties rely extensively on them to take the public pulse.

But the parties know that the results must be handled with care as there are many variables which can distort the outcome – garbage in, garbage out. In order to attempt to mirror the wider population, representative samples are chosen, but this is easier said than done.

A snapshot of one weekend in the year does not in itself provide much guidance but, if it is used as part of a trend, it can provide useful insights into public attitudes and inclinations.

Polls are simply a measurement tool; they do not explain why people believe certain things or how they can be persuaded to change their minds.

But, no matter how many precautions are taken, and how many caveats are applied to the use of the information, there is an irresistible temptation simply to look at the bottom line. The greatest culprits are journalists, always in a hurry to meet a deadline, who often use the results to provide a foundation and a cover for their views.

As one would expect in a nation of 330 million people, many

with very sophisticated skill sets, there is no shortage of "experts" in the field. Nate Silver became a celebrity because of his near infallibility in picking the results of the 2008 and 2012 elections. His subsequent book, *The Signal and the Noise*, was an instant best seller, and named by Amazon.com as the number 1 best non-fiction book of 2012.

In 2010, his 538 blog was licensed for publication by the *New York Times*. In 2012 and 2013, it won Webby Awards as the "Best Political Blog". In July 2013, Silver sold FiveThirtyEight to ESPN, and became its Editor in Chief.

Silver was named one of The World's 100 Most Influential People by *Time* in 2009 after an election forecasting system he developed successfully predicted the outcomes in 49 of the 50 states in the 2008 US Presidential election.

In the 2012 United States presidential election, Silver's forecasting system correctly predicted the winner of all 50 states and the District of Columbia. Yet, like many outlets, 538, the blog founded by Silver, failed to anticipate Donald Trump's victory in the 2016 presidential election. The 28% chance of victory it gave Trump going into election day was, however, significantly higher than that of most other analysts.

In 2020, 538 correctly predicted Joe Biden's victory in the election, forecasting 48 out of 50 states correctly.

But only a few days before the election the consensus of major national polls tracked by 538 gave Biden a stunning 8.4% lead. Moreover, it suggested that Biden would coast to victory in Florida when Trump actually won it. 538 was not alone, as the polling website RealClearPolitics' national average forecast a 7.2% lead for Biden going into the election.

In 2016 the most egregious polling error seemed to be a failure to weight by education. This led to a serious under-representation of the number of voters without a college degree, who backed Trump in huge numbers.

But even correcting for this seems to have made no difference in 2020 when both state and national polls consistently showed Biden faring far better than Trump among white voters without a degree. The results made it clear that he did not and, in many cases, he did considerably worse.

The poll results among seniors were another symptom of a deeper failure in the 2020 results. Surveys consistently showed Biden winning by comfortable margins among voters 65 and over with the final NBC/WSJ poll showing Biden 23 points ahead and the final NYT/Siena up by 10 – both wrong by large margins.

Silver and most of the polls correctly predicted that Biden would win the presidency but they were wrong in all kind of details and, a number of Senate races, badly wrong. 538 predicted that Biden would win Wisconsin by 8.3%, when he barely scraped in by less than one%. Similarly, in the Senate race in Maine, it estimated that the Democrats would win by two points; in the event they lost by nine points.

According to Salvatore Babones, an American sociologist and currently a Sydney University academic: "In the age of the mobile phone very few people answer calls from unlisted numbers, and even fewer want to talk to a pollster."

According to the Pew Research Center, response rates have plummeted from 36% two decades ago to just 9% now.

David Shor, an independent data analyst and veteran of the Obama presidential campaigns, has come to the view that the kind of people who answer polls are systematically different from the kind of people who refuse to answer polls. In other words, people who respond to polls are not a representative sample, being more likely to pick up the phone if they are Democrat supporters.

Those who refuse to answer tend to have low levels of trust in other people and tend to vote Republican. Shor concluded:

> Nearly all of the (2020) national polling error can be explained by the post-Covid jump in response rates among Dems.

According to sociologist, Robert Putnam, the tendency for people who do not trust other people to be much less likely to answer phone surveys has been around for many years. But the phenomenal rise and later day ubiquity of mobile phones at the expense of landlines has dramatically changed the equation, together with the emergence of the "shy Trump voter" phenomenon. Incidentally, the UK had experienced a "shy Tory vote" in 2015, but no one seemed to notice.

The tendency for respondents to be more inclined to answer in a manner that reflects positively on their preferred candidate and political views seems to have become much more pronounced.

Patrick Murray, director of the Monmouth University Polling Institute, says this "social desirability" bias is a phenomenon unique to Trump.

In the past, when people were asked whether they approved or disapproved of the president, the answer was usually based on performance: "Now, it's become a reflection of who you are as a person and how other people in society see you."

Democrats, particularly highly committed ones who donate to and volunteer for campaigns, are more likely to respond to polls. Especially in the midst of a pandemic, talking politics relieves boredom and feels socially useful.

It may also be that this group were home and able to take the call whereas non-respondents were more likely to be out at work or looking for it. In any event, they were reluctant to take a call from an unidentified source.

Shor also believes that people who answer surveys are "really weird", being considerably more politically engaged with higher levels of social trust and excited to share their opinions.

This constitutes a deadly challenge to a core premise of polling which assumes that you can use the response of poll takers to infer the views of the population at large and that differences can be statistically controlled by "weighting" according to social factors such as race, education and gender.

The "shy Trump voters" thesis has some validity but fundamentally the problem is not that people were not telling the truth, when asked who they were voting for, but that the wrong people were answering the surveys.

One explanation for the gross inaccuracy of the polls, especially in 2016, is that there was a silent Trump vote, analogous to the "shy Tory" vote at the UK general election in 2015. There the polls, and, obediently, the commentators, had predicted a too-close-to-call result, but the Conservatives unexpectedly won a majority in the House of Commons. A cogent reason advanced was that people did not want to tell pollsters that they were proposing to vote Conservative.

It is very plausible that, in the febrile atmosphere of the 2016 US campaign, many were afraid of being shamed if they admitted to what the politically correct media would regard as an unfathomable heresy.

There was never any prospect that such people would be outed by pollsters, but such self-protective behaviour shows the depth of concern many felt at being oppressed and browbeaten by an untrustworthy media.

Polls, particularly those conducted many months before the likely election date, when it is not "real time", are rarely a reliable guide to eventual voting intentions. This is especially so when the media uses artificial constructs such as "the nationwide polling average" as a cover to avoid doing the hard yards and digging down into the key marginals.

There is no evidence that Trump fared worse in coronavirus hotspots, contrary to the expectation of many commentators.

This is evidenced by the result in Wisconsin, one of the major hotspots where, as already noted, the polls badly underestimated Mr Trump.

One state, where the polls were most unreliable in 2020, was Florida where Trump made huge gains among Hispanic voters. In Miami-Dade County Biden won by just seven points where Clinton had won by 29 points. This was not just about Cuban-Americans. Trump made huge gains in many Hispanic communities throughout the country.

It is very easy to assume that racial factors were at work, but the more likely explanation is that these people voted the same way as millions of ordinary working class Americans, with their primary concerns being jobs, families and mortgages, a patriotic pride in their circumstances and a resentment at being treated as cannon fodder in political debates.

The *New York Times* poll expert, Nate Cohn, believes there was a bigger polling miss, leading up to the 2020 election, than in 2016: "The polls always showed the President faring better among non-white, and particularly Hispanic, voters than he did four years ago but the magnitude of the shift was way beyond expectations."

One stratagem, which figured greatly in post-mortems, was Trump's so-called "voter suppression strategy", involving expenditure of some $US 159 million of Facebook and Instagram advertisements in the final weeks of the campaign.

As voting is voluntary in the US, extraordinary time, money and effort is devoted to getting out the vote or, in this case, not. Trump's strategy in 2016 was designed to discourage Clinton supporters from voting, and was principally aimed at idealistic white liberals, young women and African Americans, identified via his digital team's customised database containing comprehensive identity profiles of 220 million Americans.

Using the Facebook "Audience Targeting Options" feature, ads could be directed at users based on their Facebook activity, ethnic affinity or location and demographics, such as age, gender and interests. In all there were around 4-5000 individual data points about the on-line and off-line life of each person.

Drawing on remarks Hillary Clinton made way back in 1996, characterising youth gangs as super predators, the Trump camp created an animation of her using the "super predator" line accompanied by text saying: "Hillary thinks African Americans are Super Predators."

Accurate or not, the tag line stuck. The idea that Trump left this type of tactic to subordinates is at odds with newspaper reports that Trump was an avid pupil who would sit on the plane alongside his digital supremo and share the latest data.

The same technique had been employed five months earlier in the July 2016 Australian Federal Election by the ALP, with its fundamentally dishonest, but nevertheless effective, Mediscare robocall assault in the last week of the campaign.

This undoubtedly had an impact in electorates such as Bass and Lyons in Tasmania, where there was a higher proportion of welfare recipients and older people fearful of any action which might increase the cost of their medical treatment or their Medicare entitlements. It should be remembered that voting in the US is voluntary, so discouraging the turnout can be effective. In Australia discouragement is not enough; to be effective it has to bring about vote switching.

The Mediscare campaign in Australia was inspired by work done by the Federal Department of Finance. It had been examining cost-saving measures such as partial outsourcing to the private sector, which Labor immediately labelled Turnbull's secret privatisation plan. That Labor has never since pursued the issue in any forum is surely proof positive that it was a fabricated election campaign tactic, not a genuine policy issue.

Even during the campaign, Bill Shorten refused to elaborate on his few one-liners, happy for them to run in subterranean fashion. There is, fortunately, a distinct downside to such sleazy tactics, especially when they do not quite succeed. Thereafter they serve as a forceful reminder of the perpetrator's inherent untrustworthiness.

The bottom line on the usability/reliability of polls is that political parties can afford the best and most reliable targeted information and are motivated to do so because they have skin in the game which the media fundamentally have not. Their principal motivation is to keep the pot boiling and not waste a lot of money on detail when most consumers are happy to be served with superficial offerings.

8

Trump: No Innocent Abroad

There is nothing on the public record to indicate that Donald Trump was a student of history, or that he had any practical foreign policy experience. Diplomatic novice as he was, he brought a fundamentally different and, in many respects, a more successful, approach to the subject than that of professional diplomats who were aghast at raw concepts such as brinksmanship.

The new art of diplomacy

In many respects, Trump relied more on instinct and argumentation than advice, which he saw as always partial, being coloured by the particular views and motives of its proponents. Drawing on his decades of experience as a high performing businessman, he brought a refreshingly commercial approach to international mediation.

In large measure this was because he eschewed the standard approach of the professionals, who heavily favoured quiet diplomacy. He saw this as a largely self-serving stratagem, enabling ambitious diplomats to move quietly up the ladder, while keeping any career-limiting mistakes out of the public eye.

More importantly, it put no pressure on other parties and was therefore ineffective. Trump may not have realised it, but he belonged to the Henry Kissinger school of diplomacy, which argued that it was necessary to gain leverage before being able to achieve significant outcomes.

Trump and the diplomatic community were never going to get on well together. They had diametrically opposed personal characteristics.

He was a bar room brawler who had spent years in the jungle of the building and construction industry, where only Rafferty's rules prevailed.

Diplomats, by contrast, were devotees of the Marquess of Queensberry's rule book, treating diplomatic conventions as iron laws. They are often judged on their polish and suavity instead of their diplomatic achievements.

They would be horrified if they gave offence, even accidentally, to friendly nations. They paid only lip service to the old English adage that nations have no permanent friends or enemies, only permanent interests.

It is highly unlikely that Trump ever thought of leaving the NATO alliance, but he knew that threats to do so were powerful weapons, as no one expected national leaders, and certainly not diplomats, to talk in such terms. The diplomats complained that he had insulted many of the leaders of America's closest friends but, again, they chose to ignore his underlying strategy which was to force "friends" to face up to the real issues, while still working closely together.

It is doubtful if any of them had read *The Art of the Deal*, in which Trump made it clear that public pressure and brinksmanship were key elements of a successful negotiation strategy.

They deplored him threatening Canada and Mexico and treating them not as friendly neighbours, but as adversaries. Again, his strategy worked and the NAFTA partners were able to restructure the agreement.

Academics and other experts asked, "what was his grand strategy", as if this was a *sine qua non* in high level diplomacy. These sorts of parlour-games might go down a treat at foreign policy workshops, but Trump was much more interested in discrete one-on-one negotiations.

Trump's rulebook and, indeed, common sense, makes it plain that it would be quite counterproductive to show your hand or disclose your ultimate intentions, so it was an exercise in futility for diplomats to ask publicly, "what is the strategy?" Still, they kept asking.

According to Western-educated Hong Kong political scientist and columnist Simon Shen:

> Like him or loathe him, Donald Trump's diplomatic achievements have been unreasonably underestimated. He is the first US president to fundamentally change the rules of international engagement since Nixon's visit to China or even since the end of World War II.

Jimmy Carter is the only other president since 1950 who did not involve the country in war, although the Congressional Research Service calculates that the US has used military force overseas 240 times during that period.

Trump went the other way, withdrawing troops from northern Syria and Afghanistan. His decision in October 2018 to pull back 1000 soldiers from observation posts in the northern Syria safe zone drew a furious reaction in some quarters but, as others quickly pointed out, if it was such an egregious error, why did the UN and/or the EU not step in to fill the void?

He was prepared to take decisive physical action on several occasions. His 2018 surgical strike on Syria was well-timed. It sent a strong message, making some amends for Obama's "red line" fiasco.

On coming to office, he almost immediately withdrew the United States from the Trans-Pacific Partnership trade deal, which the United States had itself helped to create. This may have been a calculated strategy to squeeze better terms for America, but it was probably more likely to have been reflective of his inherent distrust of multilateralism. It did not deter Australia from proceeding apace and success on this front could be a powerful exemplar in due course.

Early in his term he confronted North Korea, which had been making bellicose nuclear noises and threatening not only its near neighbours, but even the United States. His coercion also forced China to face up to the nuclear threat in its own backyard.

Trump adopted a "maximum pressure and engagement" approach, and bulked up economic sanctions, which did deliver some modest conciliatory gestures from the hermit kingdom, as well as dramatically toning down its hitherto hysterical rhetoric.

Forsaking diplomatic niceties, Trump took to labelling the North Korean leader, Kim Jong-un, "little rocket man", and raised the stakes to the point where the two leaders met for three ultimately anti-climactic summits, but which significantly diminished the level of tension.

Other early initiatives included a ban on travel from certain Muslim-majority countries and increased belligerency against Venezuela. The former had no international support but the latter had much.

According to Shen, Trump's replacement of the decades-old Asia-Pacific Strategy with an Indo-Pacific Strategy is the biggest change in US post-war geopolitics.

China

When China joined the World Trade Organization in 2002, the universal expectation was that it was the first step towards adopting the Western capitalist model and becoming a powerful and respected member of the international community. Through a succession of Chinese presidents this had remained a valid assumption. It was not until Xi Jinping ruthlessly installed himself as President for Life that the scales dropped and the West realised that China was rapidly becoming a wolf in sheep's clothing.

Whilst concerns had from time to time been voiced *sotto voce* in diplomatic circles about China's increasingly belligerent approach to several of its regional neighbours and its major trading partners, Trump was the first to confront the challenge head on.

His Indo-Pacific strategy was based on a desire to progressively decouple US dependency on China and reduce the need for smaller ASEAN nations to rely on China's seductive but insidious Belt and Road bait. His standing up to China has since been welcomed, even if somewhat timidly, by Japan, South Korea and Vietnam.

India, facing border incursions from a newly aggressive China, also had every reason to be grateful to Trump for upping the ante. The extent of high level Indian support can be gauged from a lead article in the venerable Indian English-language daily newspaper, *The Economic Times*, the voice of the Indian business establishment.

It said that Trump came to be viewed as probably the best Republican president ever and that his greatest achievement was his blunt recognition of China as the new geopolitical threat of the 21st century.

Trump not only caused the US national security establishment to turn away from decades of seeing the Middle East as the most important foreign policy issue and, instead, to focus on where the real danger was coming from – a rampant Beijing, posing an existential threat to the United States for the foreseeable future.

In particular, he drew attention to the very real prospect of China achieving global technological dominance and took multiple steps to reduce US reliance on China for critical materials.

In recent years, the biggest foreign policy issue has been China's brazen assertion of territorial rights in the South China Sea and its island militarisation strategy, both in defiance of international law.

Obama and others had complained about this but had otherwise done very little. Trump soon made it clear that he would not allow such behaviour to go unchecked, although it was still not clear what the most effective option might be.

But the most important strategic foreign policy decision of his presidency was his resolve to tackle China's global subversion of the United States and other nations: its increasingly blatant industrial-scale theft of intellectual property, its full frontal cyber-attacks on every aspect of governmental institutions and major corporations, its unashamed interference on university campuses and its clandestine recruitment of leading scholars and researchers.

It is now becoming increasingly clear that most Western nations will seek to pursue a progressive and targeted disengagement strategy whilst endeavouring to maintain lucrative trading opportunities. In leading the charge, Trump delivered a wake-up call to all leading nations, and even the European Union is now taking similar steps to confront this imminent global challenge.

Trump's guiding principles

In many ways Trump's objectives were very conventional. He sought to re-assert the supremacy of the US-led rules regime, based on international order, although not as a global policeman. His foreign policy interventions did not suggest that he was an isolationist but that he wished to shake up international relations and restore US primacy.

Paul Kelly, doyen of Australian political commentators, rightly identified Trump as seeing global politics in terms of national rivalry, not as an interdependent world issue: "He rejects notions of a liberal international order to proactively shape the world." But Trump is probably not the only gun-shy leader in the wake of the last Iraq war and other failed interventions such as Libya and Syria, with all their unintended consequences.

His less expansive, and desirably less expensive, world-view might also have reflected a belief that multilateral forums are at best likely to produce slow and weak compromises, whereas bilateral engagement provides a more effective opportunity to address competing interests, quickly and directly.

His approach probably also derived from his lifelong practice of doing one-on-one deals with counterparties. The broader takeout is that, unlike Obama, he acknowledged American exceptionalism, was proud of America's role in the world and was determined that it should continue to be the lead player on the international stage.

He was more than prepared to enhance its defence strengths to maintain US hegemony, in the face of the China challenge, while recognising that there are commensurate global responsibilities.

He emphasised action to counter the Chinese threat with ambitious plans to bulk up the US Navy dramatically to over 350 ships.

In doing all this, he demolished the fond and widely held hope that China would quietly join the global economic fold and ultimately come to embrace democratic liberalism. Trump's forthright stance and his willingness to keep tightening the screws has since effectively won world-wide Western support.

Complementing the new architecture was the US-led Quadrilateral Dialogue – a "four-nation alliance", composed of Japan, Australia and India, all solid and reliable allies. He also doubled down on support for Taiwan, with additional arms sales, and took a much harder line on Beijing's land grab in the South China Sea, which also threatens Taiwan's security.

The Middle East

Another achievement often overlooked was the Trump administration's determined and ultimately successful efforts at rolling back the Islamic State's physical caliphate and ultimately the killing of its leader, Abu Bakr al-Baghdadi, in October 2019. There had previously been much Western hand-wringing on the issue but Trump was the only one with the capacity and determination to see the challenge through.

His nixing of the flawed Iran nuclear deal was always going to be controversial, as Obama clearly saw it as one of his finest achievements. Trump had never liked Obama's nuclear deal, which he had loudly and consistently criticised for several years before coming to office. He saw the deal as having very dubious benefits for the United States and the global community, while giving Iran a huge cash hand-out, which had simply been used to increase its capacity to foment unrest in the region and continue its clandestine nuclear build up.

Instead, he introduced tougher sanctions designed to bring Iran's oil exports to zero, an exercise which was largely successful during his term; Biden now has other ideas. Most in the foreign policy establishment agreed with Trump on this and also quietly cheered at the killing of a top general and chief architect of Iran's network of dangerous militias throughout the Middle East.

Israel

Another major achievement was to defuse Middle East politics by sidestepping the intractable Palestine issue, which many countries in the region had continued to use as a domestic political card to be played rather than an issue to be solved.

His decision to move the US Embassy from Tel Aviv to Jerusalem provoked dire warnings, but even the Arab reaction was muted and, ultimately, Joe Biden came to support the initiative.

After years of Obama expressing mealy-mouthed distaste for Israel, Trump set about implementing a long-term strategy of getting much closer to Israel. By publicly reconciling Israel with the United Arab Emirates, Bahrain, Sudan, Morocco, and potentially a number of others who had previously been locked into a moribund ideological pro-Palestinian, anti-Israel position, he changed the regional dynamic.

Moderate countries came to realise the futility of not developing valuable trading and even national security opportunities with one of the very few Middle East success stories. Meanwhile, he strengthened ties with other regional leaders such as Turkey, Saudi Arabia and Egypt.

Trump had an instinctive aversion to distant, often hostile, multilateral organisations, preferring direct and personal negotiations. Hence his withdrawal from the World Health Organization, the Paris agreement on climate change and even the Trans-Pacific Partnership on free trade, which the United States had helped to create.

Climate change

His decision to withdraw from the Paris Accord on climate change was a pre-election commitment and should have come as no surprise to anyone. Yet it provoked howls of outrage from the progressive left.

Both parties in Congress had unanimously opposed the Kyoto Protocol and took the same view of the Paris Accord, which imposed no effective obligations on major emitters such as China and India, while loading heavy financial burdens on Western countries.

Trump recognised that in some ways the United Nations was seeking to turn the issue of climate change into a rerun of the 1980s North-South dialogue, a thinly disguised massive wealth transfer from rich to poor nations. He would have none of this, seeing it as yet another example of a gratuitous and unbalanced trading arrangement, while making no meaningful contribution to carbon emission reductions or the global warming debate.

Trump was more interested in practical outcomes, being very much aware that since 2005 US greenhouse gas emissions had already fallen by 13%. This was, in considerable measure, a result of his pro-fracking policy, which had massively lowered both energy costs and greenhouse gas emissions.

NATO

He was not the first president to complain about NATO members freeloading on the US defence capability. A few years back they had grudgingly agreed to increase their defence funding to 2% of GDP, but had done little about it, confident that successive presidents would only complain, but take no effective action. It was left to Trump to call their bluff.

In his inimitable style, following the template he laid down in *The Art of the Deal*, he threatened to rip up the NATO security blanket, thereby forcing its members to come to the table. Even Angela Merkel felt compelled to say that Europe needed to do more.

But there was one issue on which NATO was very supportive of America's actions. Trump's abandonment of the Intermediate-Range Nuclear Forces Treaty, after years of Russian violations, was seen as a major diplomatic achievement.

NAFTA

Closer to home, another significant initiative was "modernisation" of the North American Free Trade Agreement to correct the US trade deficit in goods with Canada and Mexico.

Once again his *Art of the Deal* instincts paid off. By his threatening to secede from NAFTA, the other parties quickly agreed to wind up existing arrangements and replace them with the United States-Mexico-Canada agreement, which came into force on 1 July 2020.

Conclusion

Even impeccable foreign policy establishment types like Robert D. Blackwill, writing on behalf of the august Council of Foreign Relations, albeit at the halfway mark in Trump's term, gave him positive marks for several of his achievements. Blackwill grudgingly concluded that, in the words of his essay's title, "Trump's Foreign Policies Are Better Than They Seem".

After the usual reservations about Trump's "dysfunctional policy-making process", Blackwill pointed to what he saw as a much-needed toughening of US policy towards China, a justified US withdrawal from Syria, disengagement from Afghanistan, and close relations with India, Israel and Saudi Arabia. There was also praise for his efforts to rally regional and international support against the Maduro regime in Venezuela.

Unfortunately, although his brief was to look at the impact of Trump's policies on the US national interest, Blackwill could not resist the temptation to devote an inordinate amount of time indulging his visceral dislike and distaste for Trump's personal qualities.

He also noted, however, the incessant torrent of abuse heaped on almost every action of the President, such as an hysterical *Foreign Policy* headline that Trump was "getting away with foreign policy insanity" – hardly a responsible assessment from a supposedly respectable source. But, as Blackwill went on to say, "these critics show no sympathy for the manifold challenges the president faces in trying to deal with a deteriorating world order that he inherited".

Blackwill also bemoaned the fact that Trump only seemed to go through the motions on consultation, while observing that his own lifelong mentor, Henry Kissinger, had achieved two major strategic breakthroughs – the opening to China and detente with the Soviet Union – with little or no relevant formal interagency process.

It remains a mystery how someone with no foreign policy expertise or experience could have successfully tackled so many big issues. The answer is likely to be that, being unburdened by any policy baggage and possessing fresh eyes, an enquiring mind and a lifetime talent for problem-solving, he was able to see solutions that others could not or did not want to see.

It is likely that we will not see Trump's like again, particularly on the international stage, but there are surely valuable insights to be derived from observing, if not emulating, some of the high wire actions of this ultimate political risk taker.

www.ingramcontent.com/pod-product-compliance
Lightning Source LLC
Chambersburg PA
CBHW031446280326
41927CB00037B/372